D0460731

Learning

Illustrator CS6

with 100 practical exercises

Learning

Illustrator CS6

with 100 practical exercises

www.mcb-press.com

Learning Illustrator CS6 with 100 practical exercises

Copyright © 2013 **MEDIAactive**

First edition: 2013

Published by © **MCB Press** owned by Marcombo. Distributed in USA and Canada by ATLAS BOOKS, 30 Amberwood Parkway, Ashland, Ohio 44805. To contact a representative, please e-mail us at order@bookmasters.com.

www.mcb-press.com

Cover Designer: Ndenu

ISBN: 978-84-267-1900-3

DL: B-20393-2013

Printed in EU

Printed by Publidisa

Presentation

LEARNING ILLUSTRATOR CS6 WITH 100 PRACTICAL EXERCISES

This book provides 100 practical exercises that take you for a tour of the main functions of the program. While it is impossible to collect all the features of Illustrator CS6 in the pages of this book, we have chosen the most interesting and useful ones. Once you have completed the 100 exercises that make up this book, you will be able to use the program and design elaborate arrangements for digital and print, both professionally and personally, with ease.

THE WAY TO LEARN

Our experience in the field of education has lead us to design this manual, where every function is learned by carrying out a practical exercise. The exercises are explained step-by-step and click by click, to leave no doubts in the execution of the process. In addition, the exercises are illustrated with descriptive images of the most important steps or the results that should be obtained, and also with IMPORTANT boxes that provide further information on each of the topics covered in the exercises.

This system ensures that upon completion of the 100 exercises that make up this manual, the user will be able to cope comfortably with the basic tools of Illustrator CS6 and get the best out of them.

FILES REQUIRED

If you want to use the sample files that appear in this book, they can be downloaded from www.mcb-press.com.

WHO SHOULD READ THIS MANUAL

If you are starting to practice and work with Photoshop, you will find a complete tour of the main functions in these pages. However, if you are an expert on the program, this manual will also be very useful to see more advanced aspects or review specific functions, which you can find in the contents section.

Each exercise is treated independently, so it is not necessary to do them in order (although we recommend it, since we have attempted to group exercises thematically). Thus, if you need to address a specific issue, you will be able to go directly to the exercise where the issue is delt with and carry it out on your own computer.

ILLUSTRATOR CS6

Illustrator CS6 is, undoubtedly, one of the more used graphic design application. The intuitive operation of this program have made it the best choice to design on the computer.

The CS6 version presents interesting news in features and tools, like the Adobe Mercury Performance System incredible to work with large, complex files with great speed and accuracy. It also includes new options like creating patterns, the tracing image, the gradient of strokes, improved Gaussian blur and integrated editing panels. But surely the most obvious improvement is the new interface, more efficient, flexible and according to the current needs.

How *Learning...* books work

The title of each exercise concisely expresses what it is about. Thus, if you are interested, you can go directly to the action you want to learn or review.

The exercises have been written systematically step-by-step, so that you will never get lost during their execution.

The number to the right of the page tells you clearly in what exercise you are.

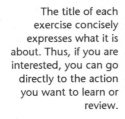

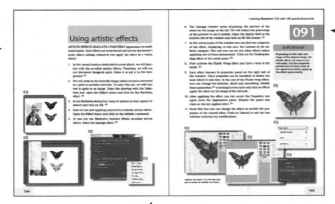

Important boxes include actions to be completed in that order to ensure that you perform the exercise correctly. They also contain information that is interesting to learn as it will facilitate your work with the program.

At the bottom of every page you can follow the exercise graphically and step-by-step. The numbers in the captions refer to entries in the main text.

Table of contents

Table of contents

Discovering the workspace

IMPORTANT

The **workspaces** of the various Adobe applications look the same such as the panels, bars, and menus; therefore, it is easy to move from one application to the next.

ADOBE ILLUSTRATOR CS6 provides a work area and a really effective user interface to create and edit artwork, which may be printed as well as published on the Internet or on mobile devices.

1. Open the **Start** menu, click on the **All Programs** directory, locate the Adobe Master Collection folder and click on **Adobe Illustrator CS6**.

2. The application opens and automatically displays its new optimized interface 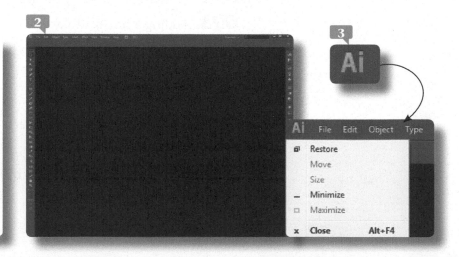 with an integrated edition in the layer names, swatches, brushes, art boards, and other panels directly in the panels themselves without using intermediary dialog boxes.

3. The Illustrator CS6 workspace is organized to give the maximum room to the central area. At the top of the interface, you can find the **Application Bar**, which is unified in a single area. There you can find the Adobe Illustrator logo on the left, and you can click on this command to have a look at the options it contains. At the right you can find the **Menu Bar**, access to Adobe Bridge, a command designed to organize open documents, a workspace switcher (which is a very interesting command and will be discussed in detail in the following exercise), a search box, and the three typical but-

1

Adobe
Adobe Master Collection CS6
- Au Adobe Audition CS6
- Br Adobe Bridge CS6
- $ Adobe ExtendScript Toolkit CS6
- Adobe Extension Manager CS6
- Fw Adobe Fireworks CS6
- Adobe Flash Professional CS6
- Ai Adobe Illustrator CS6
- Adobe InDesign CS6
- Adobe Media Encoder CS6
- Ps Adobe Photoshop CS6
- Pl Adobe Prelude CS6

2

3

Ai

| Ai | File | Edit | Object | Type |

- Restore
- Move
- Size
- Minimize
- Maximize
- x Close   Alt+F4

tons to minimize, maximize or restore, and close the program window.

4. Below the **Menu Bar** you can find the area of the control panel that constantly adapts to the selected tool in the **Tools** panel, which is vertically arranged to the left of the workspace. To display the tools in a single column, click on the double arrow at the top left of the panel.

5. The vertical dock panel groups are located to the right of the workspace. To expand or contract them, click on the head of the double cursor.

6. If you do not have any document open on the screen, all panels are displayed in gray. To move from one panel to another, simply click on their tabs. Illustrator's interface is fully customizable, which means that you can hide and display panels that interest you the most. To do this, open the **Window** menu and click on the **Color** option.

7. The **Color** panel has disappeared from the interface. As you work with the program, you will find out which panels you use the most and the least. To the right of each panel there is a button with three horizontal stripes, which opens the options for each panel. Finish this exercise by contracting the panels to icons by clicking on the button with a double-headed cursor.

001

IMPORTANT

The panel groups have an icon on their top bar containing a menu with options to manage them.

Swatches   Brushes   Symbols

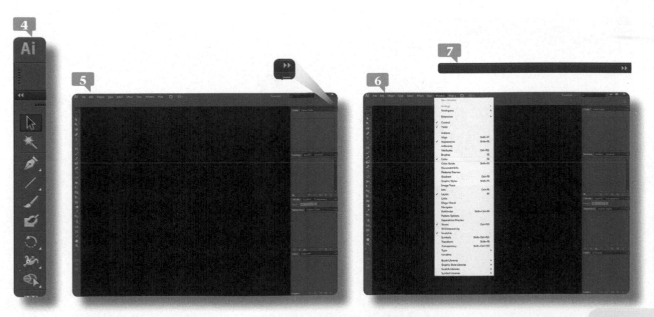

Customizing the workspace

ILLUSTRATOR CS6 FEATURES a default workspace. However, if you prefer, you can customize the program to your way of working by selecting one of several preset workspaces or by creating your own customized one.

1. The default workspace of Illustrator CS6 is called **Essentials** and can be found on the right side of the **Application Bar**. Click on the cursor of this command to have a look at its contents.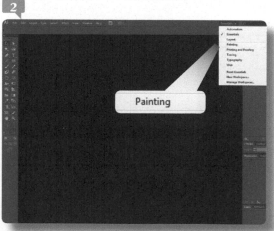

2. Illustrator allows you to modify the workspace to different, previously established uses such as design, color, typography, etc. As an example, click on the command **Painting**.

3. The workspace changes instantly 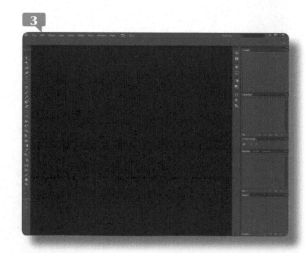 by adapting to the tools and the disposition of the bars and panels that are used in this type of task. Each of the options displays the most appropriate and most often used tool in each of the default options.

4. The new workspace displays those panels that are used in this type of task. The fact that the other panels are not displayed does not mean that they cannot be used. Open the **Window**

Essentials

Painting

002

menu, click on the **Appearance** panel or click on the icon in the vertical panel groups (in this case the icon that looks like a sun).

5. Knowledge on how to customize workspaces is a huge advantage, since you can save them. To save the current space, expand the field of the Application bar that now displays the word **Painting** and click on the command **New Workspace**.

6. The **New Workspace** dialog box opens, where you need to enter a name. For example, type in the term **painting2** and press the **OK** button.

7. Note that the field in the Application Bar displays the name of the personal space. In order to show you how you can access a personalized space, you need to go back to the defaults in Illustrator. This time, you are accessing it from the **Window** menu. Open this menu, click on the **Workspace** command and select the **Essentials** option.

8. The interface is reorganized and displays the same panels of the initial configuration. Finally, open the **Workspaces** field in the Application Bar and check if the **painting2** personalized space appears in the menu.

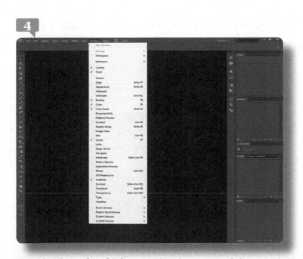

The check mark, which precedes the name of the panels, indicates that they are active on the screen.

Creating documents

A DOCUMENT IS THE SPACE in which you can create an artwork. In Illustrator, you can create documents destined for different types of outputs: printing, web, mobile devices, video, and film, etc.

1. In this exercise you will create a new document from scratch, which is based on one of the Illustrator templates. Open the **File** menu and click on the **New** command.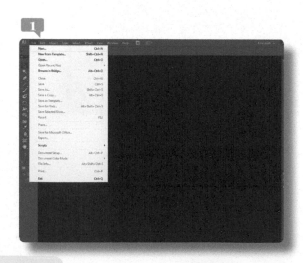

2. This opens the **New Document** dialog box, in which you need to specify the name as well as the document profile according to the predicted output. In the **Name** field, type **Project 1**.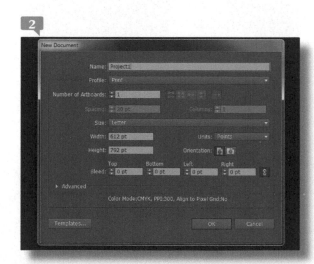

3. In the **New Document Profile** field, check if the **Print** option is selected, which involves a series of predetermined characteristics. These characteristics adapt according to the selected profile. To check this, deploy this field and select, for example, the **Web** option.

4. The fields adapt to the selected profile. Since you want to keep the default profile, open the same field again and select the **Print** option.

5. The **Number of Artboards** field was new in Illustrator CS4. Artboards represent the regions that can contain printable art-

work from the same document. By default, all new documents are created with just one artboard. But as you know, you can choose up to 100 artboards and arrange them in different ways. In the next exercise, we will discuss the usefulness of artboards. Keep all options as they are set to default and click on **OK** to create the new document.

6. The new blank document opens on the screen. 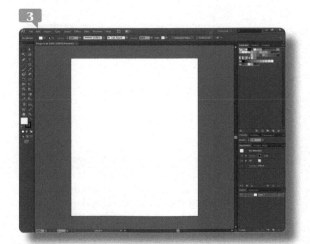 You now have the opportunity to check the adaptable content of the Options Bar, which can be found below the **Menu Bar**, and the appearance of the **Status Bar** at the bottom of the program window. The tabbed document view contains a fast and direct way to move from one document to another. You will create a second document, but this time it will be based on a template. To do this, open the **File** menu and click on the **New from Template** command.

7. The **New from Template** dialog box opens, in which you need to select the template you want to use. As you can see, the program offers a number of templates organized according to the topic and type. As an example, double-click on the **Blank templates** folder, select the **T-shirt** template  and click on the **New** button.

The new document based on the template is loaded into the workspace of the application and ready to be edited.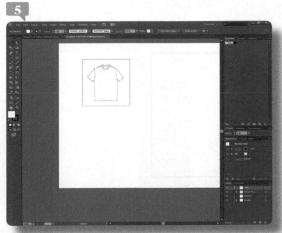

003

IMPORTANT

At the bottom left of the New Document dialog box is the **Advanced** button, which extends the table with three options: **Color Mode**, **Raster Effects**, and **Preview Mode**.

▸ Advanced

4

- Brochure.ait
- Business Cards.ait
- Cards and Invitations.ait
- CD Cases.ait
- CD Print Items.ait
- Gift Certificate Pouchette.ait
- Labels.ait
- Promotional 1.ait
- Promotional 2.ait
- Stationery.ait
- Tshirt.ait
- Website and DVDMenu.ait

Any personalized document can be saved as a template to be reused as many times as necessary.

3

5

Designing with artboards

ARTBOARDS REPRESENT THE REGIONS that can contain printable artwork from the same document. You can use artboards as crop areas for printing or placing purposes. The Artboard panel in Illustrator CS6 allows you to add, rearrange, and reorder, as well as duplicate artboards within the panel.

1. Click on the tab of the **Project1** document in order to place it in the foreground.

2. This document contains one single artboard. In the **Tools** panel, you need to click on the **Artboard** icon, which is displayed as a square with crop marks.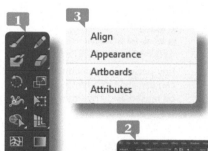

3. The appearance of the workspace changes to display the existing artboard, which is enclosed by a dotted line. You can create a new artboard without creating a new document and specify this feature in the **New Document** box from the new **Artboards** panel. Open the **Window** menu and click on the **Artboards** option.

4. Press the Options button in the new **Artboards** panel and select the **New Artboard** option.

The Options panel displays all necessary commands to edit this item when you activate the Artboard tool.

You can also create new artboards by dragging them while holding down the Alt key, which creates a duplicate artboard.

5. A small box with the value 2 is displayed in the upper left corner of the new artboard, which indicates that two artboards are now available. According to the content you want to edit in the artboard, you can change the size upward or downward. Although the proportions can be changed directly in the Options panel of the **Artboard** tool, you need to access the Properties box of this element. Press the Options button of the **Artboard** panel and select **Artboard Options**.

6. You need to halve the size of the table 2. Click on the **Constrain proportions** check box so that as you change one of the measured values the other one adjusts proportionally.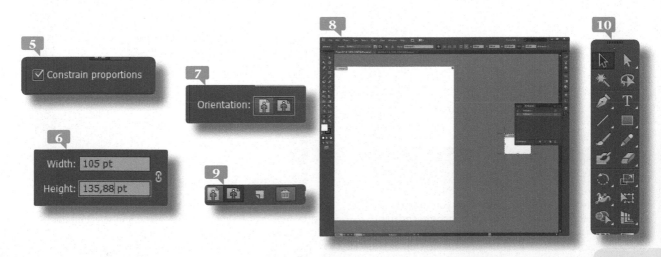

7. Then type **105** the **Width** field and click on the **Height** field to see how it adapts proportionally to its content.

8. You also need to change the orientation of the artboard. Click on the second icon in the **Orientation** section to change to a horizontal orientation and press **OK** to adjust the new artboard.

9. Hide the **Artboards** panel by clicking on the double-headed arrow.

10. Remove the second artboard. Select this artboard, click on the **Delete Artboard** option, which is displayed as a trash can in the **Options Bar**, and return to the normal view by clicking on the first icon in the **Tools** panel.

IMPORTANT

The position of the artboard can be either modified from the **Artboard Options** by entering the preferred values in the X and Y field or by dragging the artboard into the workspace.

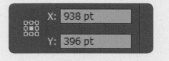

X: 938 pt

Y: 396 pt

Page size and orientation

When creating a new document, it is possible to specify the page size (width and height) as well as its orientation in the **New document** dialog box.

BY DEFAULT, ILLUSTRATOR CS6 ADJUSTS all new documents to the document profile for Print A4 paper type. This type of paper has a width of 210 mm and a height of 297 mm vertically.

1. This simple exercise will show you how to change the size and orientation of a previously created document. Open the document you created in the **T-Shirt** template exercise.

2. You need to change the page display so that you can see the entire page. In the Status Bar, click on the first field, which displays the current zoom percentage, and select the option **Fit On Screen**.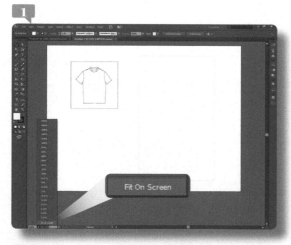

3. As you can see, this document has a landscape orientation. To access the Properties box, click on the command **Document Setup** in the **Options Bar** while selecting the first tool in the panel.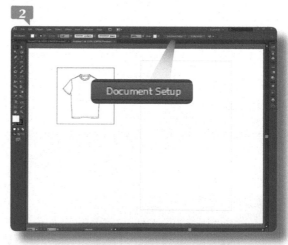

4. This opens the **Document Setup** dialog box, which consists of three sections: **Bleed and View Options**, **Transparency**, and **Type Options**. Keep the measurement unit as millimeters

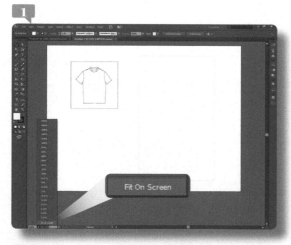

The long list of the zoom values allows you to select a percentage of up to 6400%, which is recommendable in those cases where you want to work in detail.

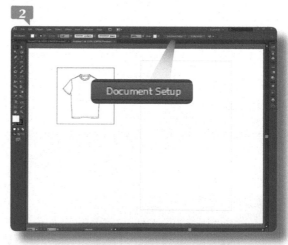

Another way to get to the **Document Setup** box is by means of opening the **File** menu and selecting the Document Setup option.

and change the values of the bleed. The bleed is the space between the edge of the paper and the content. Double-click on the **Top** field in the **Bleed** section, enter a value of **8**, and then click on the next field.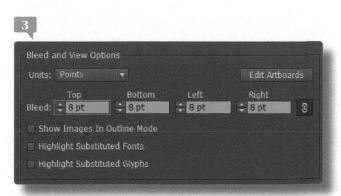

5. If you did not enable the icon next to the **Right** field, the other bleed fields will be updated with the same value. Since we have not shown you yet how to work with the grid, you need to keep the values of the Transparency section as they appear by default. As for the Type options, do not modify them. Click on **OK** to apply the change to the bleed.

6. You will have noticed that the orientation parameters were not part of the **Document Setup** box. This is because this can be adjusted in the artboard mode. To change the orientation of your document, click on the **Artboard** tool in the **Tools** panel.

7. You can now access the Options box of the artboard and change the orientation from the Options Bar respectively, as you will see below. Click on the **Vertical** command, which is located to the right of the field that displays the term A4, and observe how the document is instantly updated.

8. Do not save the changes to the current document. Click on the "x" in the document tab and press **NO** in the dialog box that asks you for confirmation to save your changes.

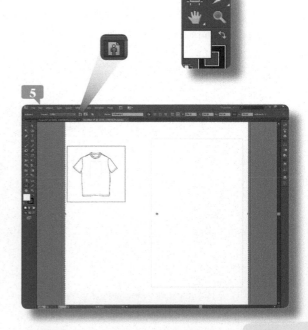

The button **Edit Artboards** in the Document Setup box allows you to access this mode and modify the preferences.

Using rulers, guides, and grid

ILLUSTRATOR CONTAINS A NUMBER of elements that help users to measure and place items within their images with total accuracy. These elements are the rulers, guides, and the grid, which are all hidden by default.

1. The rulers help you accurately place and measure objects within the illustration window or in an artboard. The point where 0 appears on each ruler is called the ruler origin. Let's see how to display the document rulers. Open the **View** menu, click on the **Rulers** command then select **Show Rulers**.

2. As you can see, the rulers of the document appear at the top and on the left side of the illustration window. 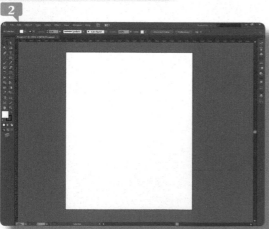 The default ruler origin is located in the lower-left corner of the illustration window. The default measure units in Illustrator are millimeters and points (one point equals 0.3528 mm). You can change the units Illustrator uses to general measures, such as lines and text. To do this, open the **Edit** menu, click on the **Preferences** command and select the **Units** option.

3. The **Stroke** and **Type** options are measured in points and the **General** option is preseted in millimeters. In this case, and for an easier handling of the measures, change the **Stroke** and

Show Rulers	Ctrl+R
Change to Global Rulers	Alt+Ctrl+R
Show Video Rulers	

006

Type options to **Millimeters** and then press the **OK** button to accept the changes.

4. The guides help you align text and graphic objects, and like the grid, they won't be printed. When the rulers of the document are activated, the guides are also enabled, but they are not displayed until they are applied to the document. Try it: Click on the vertical ruler, hold down the mouse button, drag the pointer into the approximate center of the document.

5. Do the same with the horizontal ruler to place a horizontal guide in the document.

6. The guides are displayed by a continuous line and in a default color. You can modify these features if desired. To do this, open the **Edit** menu, click on the **Preferences** command and select the **Guides & Grid** option.

7. From here you can modify the properties of the guides and the grid. Choose whether you want a different Color and apply a points Style to have a look at the difference.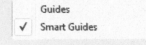

8. To remove the guides added to a document simply press the **backspace** key after selecting them. If you want to delete them all, open the **View** menu, click on the **Guides** command and select the **Clear Guides** option.

9. Before finishing off, we will also explain the grid. The grid appears behind the illustration in the illustration window and does not print. Open the **View** menu and select the **Show Grid** option.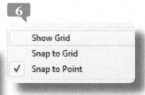

IMPORTANT

Illustrator contains the so-called Smart Guides, which are active by default. These are temporary adjustment guides that appear when you create or manipulate objects or artboards, and they help you to align, edit, and transform objects or artboards relative to other objects, artboards, or both by snap-aligning and displaying the delta and location values of X and Y.

	Guides
✓	Smart Guides

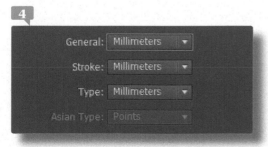

The **General** measurement option affects rulers, measuring the distance between points, moving and transforming objects, setting grid and guide spacing, and creating shapes.

Guides can be moved, hidden, and deleted once they are placed in the document. To move them, you simply need to use the drag technique, and to hide or remove them you can use the commands in the View menu.

You can drag objects to the guides to facilitate their insertion into documents. To do this, open the View menu and select the **Snap to point** option.

Varying the background of a document

IMPORTANT

Do not mix up the grid destined for the alignment and placement of objects in the document with the transparency grid, which you are working with in this exercise, and which can be used to configure the aspects of the document background with respect to the objects that are part of it.

BY DEFAULT, ILLUSTRATOR DISPLAYS ALL DOCUMENTS with a white background. This background can be modified by using basic and customized colors. However, it is necessary to choose background colors that do not impede the visualization of other elements, objects, and text that make up the picture.

1. You need to modify the document by hiding the grid, which was explained in the previous exercise, so you can see the result. To do this, open the **View** menu and click on the **Hide Grid** command.

2. Display the **View** menu again and click on the **Show Transparency Grid** option.

3. The transparency grid is used to identify the transparent areas of the illustration. However, this grid can be adjusted so that it can be used as the background color of the document. To change these features, click on the **Document Setup** button in the **Options Bar**. (Make sure that you have not selected any guide.)

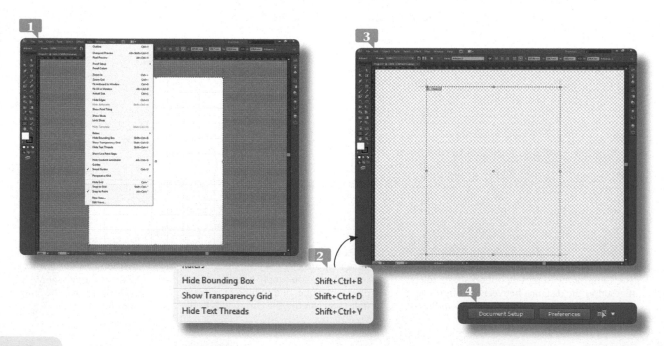

Hide Bounding Box	Shift+Ctrl+B
Show Transparency Grid	Shift+Ctrl+D
Hide Text Threads	Shift+Ctrl+Y

Document Setup   Preferences

007

4. This opens the **Document Setup** dialog box that we worked with in previous exercises. This box contains the **Transparency** section in which you need to carry out the changes to set the background color of the document. Click on the **Simulate Colored Paper** check box to enable it.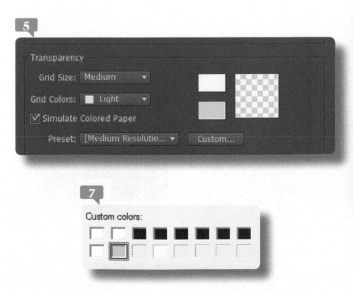

5. The **Simulate Colored Paper** option is useful if you plan to print the document on colored paper. For example, if you draw a blue object on a yellow background, the object will be green. The simulation is only carried out if the transparency grid is not displayed. Open the **Grid colors** field.

6. Check that the program provides some basic default colors, and that it also allows you to select colors from a vast palette. Simply click on the **Custom** option that appears.

7. This opens the **Color** dialog box, where you can select a color from the **Basic Colors** palette or choose a less defined color in the box to the right. In this case, select a very light blue hue, click on the **Add to Custom Colors** button and click **OK**.

8. In the **Color** box of the grid boxes, select the same color in the **Custom colors** section and press the **OK** button.

9. Press the **OK** button in the **Document Setup** dialog box and have a look at the result.

10. Open the **View** menu and click on the **Hide Transparency Grid** option.

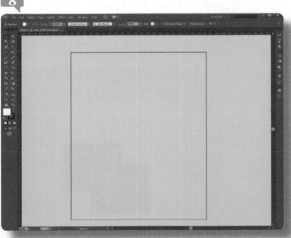

You can also change the color of the artboard to simulate the look of the picture as if it were printed on colored paper.

Selecting objects with the Selection Tool

ILLUSTRATOR ALLOWS YOU to select one or more objects in a document individually or in groups in order to edit them. To do this, you can use a few different tools. The most basic one is the Selection Tool.

1. In this exercise you will learn how to select objects individually or in groups. In order to select any object you need to have the **Selection Tool** enabled, which is the first command in the **Tools** panel. Since you have not drawn any image yet, we recommend that you download the file named **Cover.ai** from our website and open it in the Illustrator workspace. Once you have done this, click on the star-shaped object.

2. An outline with small boxes called anchor points appears around the object to indicate that it has been selected. These anchor points help you to increase or decrease the size and change its direction, as we will show you later on. Check if the **Options Bar** has adapted to the characteristics of the object. To deselect the object, you can press the **Esc** key or click on a free area of the document.

3. Click on the right of the star to deselect it. You can also deselect an object at the same time as you select another object.

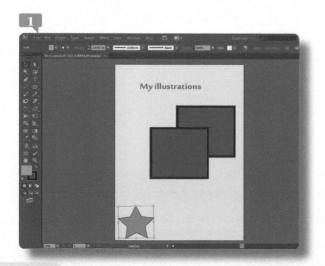

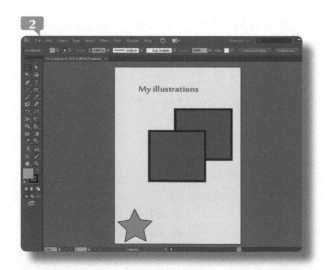

To do this, you just need to select the two objects successively. Click on the top square.

4. Click on the lower square.

5. See how the first image you have selected got deselected, and the second image maintains its selection. If you want to maintain the selection of multiple objects in a document, you need to press the **Shift** key while clicking on them. Press the **Shift** key and without releasing it, click on the top square.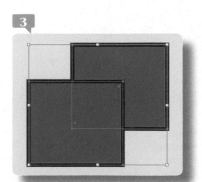

6. Now both images are selected. To deselect, click on a free area of the document.

7. Sometimes you need to select all elements on a page. In this case it would take up too much time to select them all individually with the **Shift** key. In order to solve this problem, open the **Select** menu and click on the command **All**.

8. At the beginning of the **Options Bar** you can now see the words **Mixed Objects,** which means that it will not be possible to display all the options of that bar, because they are different.  Imagine you are now interested in excluding one of the objects from the selection. In cases like this, you can also use the **Shift** key. Press this key and click on the star in order to delete the current selection. 5

9. Joint editing is one of the applications of the group selection. For example, you can move all selected items in one block. Repeatedly press the **down arrow** key on your keyboard and see how the selected elements move toward the bottom.

10. Click on a free area of the page to delete the selection.

008

IMPORTANT

Another way to select several elements that are located in the same area of a document is by using the drag technique. Draw a rectangle which completely covers the objects that are part of the selection with the help of the **Selection** Tool.

3

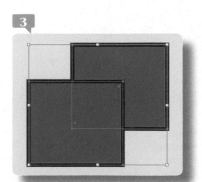

4

Another way to select all drawn elements in a document is by pressing the key combination **Ctrl + A.**

5

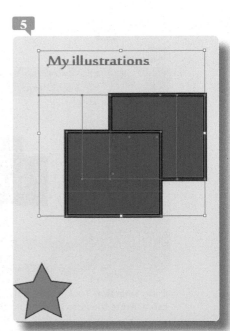

The Lasso and Magic Wand Tools

IMPORTANT

The **Magic Wand Tool** can be customized in many ways. To do this, double-click on this tool in the **Tools** panel to open the **Magic Wand** panel. You can also access this panel by opening the **Window** menu and clicking on the **Magic Wand** option.

Links

Magic Wand

THE LASSO TOOL ALLOWS YOU TO SELECT OBJECTS, anchor points or path segments by dragging around the object or a part of it, whereas the Magic Wand Tool helps you to select objects of the same color, stroke weight, stroke color, opacity, or blending mode.

1. In this exercise, you will use the two selection tools that are applicable according to the type of object you want to select. These two tools are called the **Magic Wand Tool** and the **Lasso Tool** and they are both included in the **Tools** panel. Click on the **Lasso Tool**, the fourth tool in the left-hand Tools group. 🔲

2. Make sure that the mouse pointer changes to an arrow next to the image of a lasso. The **Lasso Tool** is applied around the object you want to select with the help of the drag technique. In this case, click on the star and, without releasing the mouse button, start to draw a line around this object. 🔲 Release the mouse button and have a look at the result. 🔲

3. As you release the mouse button, the star is delimited by a number of anchor points that allow you to modify the shape

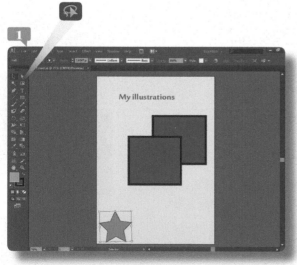

If the **Selection** Tool in the **Tools** panel is enabled, you can activate the lasso by pressing the **Q** key.

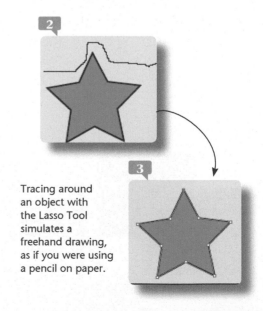

Tracing around an object with the Lasso Tool simulates a freehand drawing, as if you were using a pencil on paper.

of the object. Check if the Options Bar displays a range of parameters for these modification elements. As an example, and since we will be working later in detail with anchor points, click on the second selection tool in the **Tools** panel, which displays a white arrow, ⬛ click on one of the star's anchor points and, without releasing the mouse button, drag it to deform the object. ⬛

4. Click on a free area of the page to deselect the deformed object. Then let's see how the **Magic Wand** selection tool works. This tool is used to select all objects in a document with the same or similar fill attributes (such as color and pattern). In the **Tools** panel, click on the already mentioned tool, the third in the selection group. ⬛

5. The mouse pointer changes into the shape of a magic wand. Click on the inside of the rectangle and see what happens. ⬛

6. The two elements that display this fill color have automatically been selected. Imagine the time you can save when working with images with many different objects. Now you can change the features of these objects by completing one action. To finish this exercise, click on a free area of the document with the **Selection Tool.** ⬛

009

IMPORTANT

In the **Magic Wand** panel, you can personalize this tool. There, the low tolerance values select objects that are very similar to the object you click, and the higher tolerance values select objects with a wider range of the selected property.

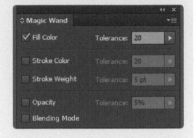

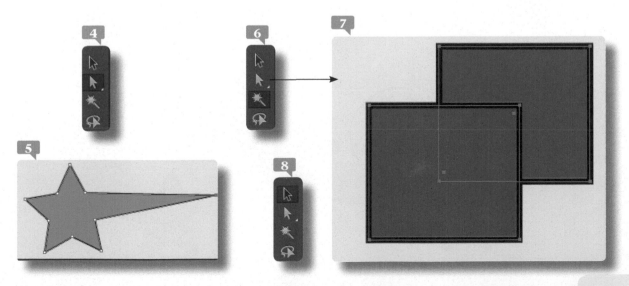

Moving and rotating objects

IN ORDER TO MOVE AN OBJECT within an Illustrator document, you can use three methods: the drag technique, the arrow keys, or the coordinates. Also, to turn or rotate an object you can also use the drag technique or modify the values of the appropriate field in the Options Bar. In both cases, it will be necessary to select the relevant tool.

1. In this exercise we will show you how to move and rotate an object. You will work with the star in the document **Cover.ai**. Start by using the drag technique. Enable the **Selection Tool**, click on the star and, without releasing the mouse button, move it slightly to the right. Release the mouse button.

2. Another way to move an object within the workspace is by using the arrow keys. To do this, you need to select the object you want to move and press the appropriate arrow keys to move the object in one direction or another. Select the star and press the right arrow key several times.

3. In this way, the object moves very slowly. There is, however, a way of moving objects longer distances with the arrow keys: by using the **Shift** key. Press the **Shift** key and, without releasing it, press the right arrow key several times.

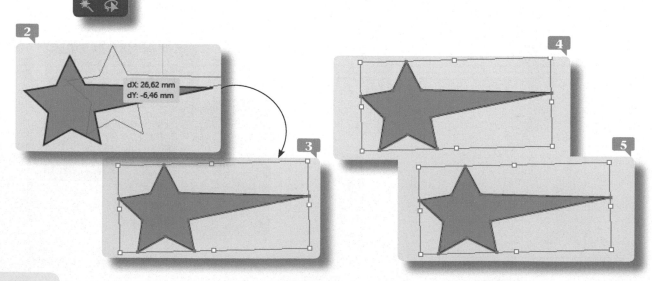

dX: 26,62 mm
dY: -6,46 mm

32

010

4. As you can see, the keystroke of the **Shift** key doubles the distance traveled. A third way of moving an object is by using the coordinates, which is only used when working with precision. The coordinates, which display the location of the objects in the document, can be found in the **Transform** panel and are accessible from the **Options Bar**. Click on the link and, ⬛ in the **Transform** panel, enter the value **160** in the X field, ⬛ which represents the horizontal plane of the object, and click on **Return**. The object has been moved to the indicated point.

5. You can also rotate an object around an axis. In the **Tools** panel, click on the **Rotate Tool,** which is displayed by a curved arrow pointing to the left. ⬛

6. As with the displacement of objects, the rotation can also be carried out by the drag technique or by entering the appropriate values. Click on the tip of the deformed star and, without releasing the mouse button, drag it up until the object is rotating. ⬛

7. The **Transform** panel also contains a field (called **Rotate**) to indicate a more precise turn of objects. In the **Options Bar**, click on the **Transform** link.

8. In the panel of the same name, enter the value **90** in the first field of the last row, ⬛ which displays the image of an angle, and press **Return** again to see how the object is once again rotated. ⬛

9. With the **Selection Tool,** click on a free area of the document to finish this exercise.

IMPORTANT

Once you have activated the Rotate Tool, the **Shift** key can also be used to rotate objects in 45° increments.

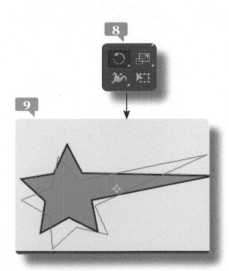

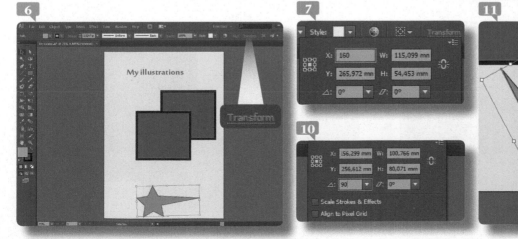

Varying the scale and shearing objects

THE MOMENT YOU CHANGE THE SCALE OF AN OBJECT, its size increases or decreases in the horizontal plane, the vertical plane, or in both. The objects are scaled with respect to a reference point that varies depending on the scaling method choosen.

1. In this exercise we will show you how to scale an object. Begin scaling by selecting the **Cover.ai** file with which you have already worked. Click on the square in the foreground.

2. Then in the **Tools** panel, select the **Scale Tool,** which is displayed by a rectangle with an arrow inside.

3. You can scale the object relative to a central point or to a specific reference point. First, you will scale relative to the central point. To do this, click on the anchor points in the lower left corner, hold down the mouse button, drag toward the center, and thereby reduce the size of the object.

4. The square size has decreased. However, note that the line, that is the black frame around it, continues to display the same thickness. To mitigate this effect so that the strokes also change the scale with the objet, you need to adjust one of the program preferences. Press the key combination **Ctrl + Z** to undo the scaling.

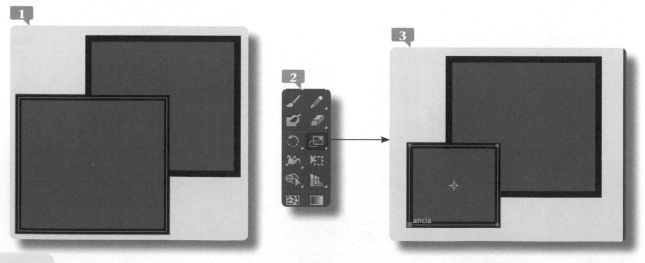

5. Open the **Edit** menu, click on the **Preferences** command and select **General**.

6. In the **Preferences** dialog box, select the **Scale Strokes & Effects** check box and press the **OK** button to apply the change.

7. To verify the change you have just specified, modify the scale relative to the reference point of the object. The reference point is the small spotlight that is in this case situated in the center of the square. To change the scale relative to this point, click on the inside of the square and, without releasing the mouse button, drag the pointer down a couple of centimeters. ⁵

8. Have a look at the difference with the scaling relative to the central point performed in the previous steps. In this case, the size change is not proportional. Now, as specified in the Preferences box, the stroke has also been scaled, as you can see in the **Stroke** field of the **Options Bar**. Before finishing this exercise, we want to show you how to shear an object. Shearing an object tilts or distorts it along the horizontal or vertical axis, or a specified angle that is relative to a specified axis. Select the rectangle, click on the cursor of the **Scale Tool** in the **Tools** panel and choose the **Shear Tool** from the list. ⁶

9. Click on the upper right anchor point, hold the mouse button and drag it to the right. ⁷

10. Select the **Selection** Tool and click on a free area of the document to deselect the sheared object.

In order to maintain the proportions of the object as you scale it, hold down the **Shift** key as you drag it.

Copying and duplicating

ILLUSTRATOR ALLOWS YOU TO COPY and duplicate objects. Although at first glance the two actions may look similar, they are not the same. When you copy an object, you create a new one with the same features, but it can be manipulated independently, whereas the duplicate of an object retains many of the original's features, but not all of them.

1. In order to perform this exercise, you can use the sample file, **Vase.ai**, which you can find in the download area of our website. Once you have copied this file to your Documents folder, open it and select the yellow flower with the **Selection Tool.**

2. Open the **Edit** menu and select **Copy.**

3. The copied object is stored on the clipboard of your computer and can be pasted into any other compatible program. This time we will paste it in the same document. To do this, open the **Edit** menu again and select the **Paste** option.

4. The new object is placed in the center of the page and is ready to be moved wherever needed. In this case, you will change its position by using the **Transform** panel. Remember that you can also do it by using the drag technique. Click on the

You can copy an object after selecting it by pressing the key combination Ctrl + C.

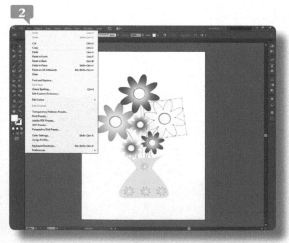

You can also paste it in another or the same document by pressing the key combination Ctrl + V.

012

Transform link in the **Options Bar** in order to open the already mentioned panel.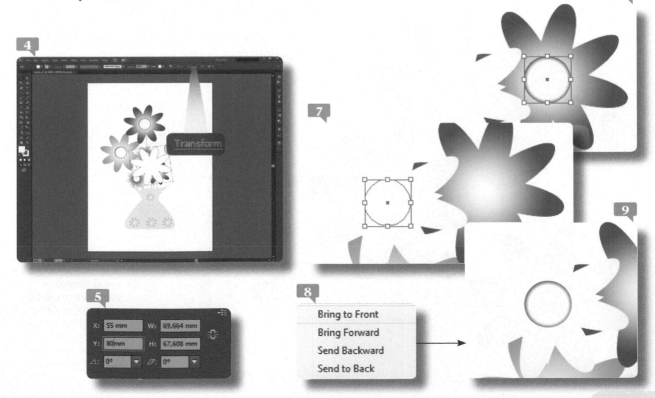

5. In the **Transform** panel, enter the value **55** in the X field, which refers to the horizontal axis, and enter the value **80** in the Y field, which refers to the vertical axis.

6. You now have a copy of the object in a different position other than the original. Duplicate a new element, which is even easier than copying objects. Select one of the circles that represent the center of the flowers.

7. Enable the **Selection Tool**, press the **Alt** key and, without releasing it, drag the shape to the left to place it in the center of the pasted flower.

8. You already have the duplicate of the original, although it is located below the flower. To display it above, open the **Object** menu, click on the **Arrange** option and select **Bring to Front**. (You will get to know the organizational options in depth in another exercise.)

9. Deselect the object by clicking on a free area of the document and complete the exercise by saving the changes— pressing the key combination **Ctrl + S**.

X: 55 mm   W: 69,664 mm
Y: 80mm   H: 67,808 mm
∆: 0°   ∅: 0°

Bring to Front
Bring Forward
Send Backward
Send to Back

Expanding, grouping, and ungrouping

OBJECTS IN AN ILLUSTRATOR DOCUMENT work independently. But sometimes different objects for some reason are related to each other within the same document and we need to modify them equally. In these cases it can be useful to create a group of objects.

1. In this exercise, you will learn how to group and ungroup objects. We will be practicing again with the **Vase.ai** file (although you know you can use your own documents if you want to.) Click on one of the flowers with the **Selection Tool**.

2. You need to select all elements that are supposed to be part of the group. In this case you want to group parts of the flower. To do this, press the **Shift** key and click on the circle that represents the center of the chosen flower and the path that represents its stem.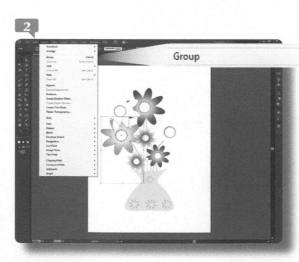

3. You can include as many elements as you want in the selection. Open the **Object** menu and click on the **Group** command.

4. Now you have grouped the three selected elements. Click on a free area of the document to delete the selection.

5. See how the three elements form a group by clicking on one of them again.

Group   Ctrl+G

In addition to the usage of the Object menu command, you can also use the context menu after selecting the elements or press the key combination **Ctrl + G** to group objects.

6. The advantage of working with grouped elements is that you can change the common properties with a single action and, for example, move them in one group. Try it: open the **Transform** panel by clicking on the corresponding link in the **Options Bar**. 3

7. Change the position of the objects by changing the values of the X and Y fields and press the **Return** key. 4

8. The three figures are moved simultaneously. As you are now no longer interested in maintaining a group of objects, you can ungroup them. To do this, click the right mouse button on the group and select the **Ungroup** option (this option can be found in the context menu). 5

9. Now we will show you how to expand an object. The expansion process allows you to divide a single object into various objects that make up its appearance (fill, stroke, etc.). In this case, click on one of the circles, 6 open the **Object** menu and select the **Expand** option.

10. The **Expand** dialog box appears, in which you can select the elements you want to separate. In this case, you can see that the Fill option is checked. Keep it checked and click on **OK** to proceed with the division. 7

11. Check in the **Options Bar** if the object is treated like a group. Click on the outside of the selection to finish this exercise.

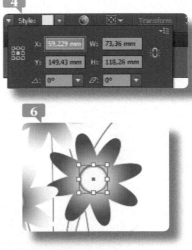

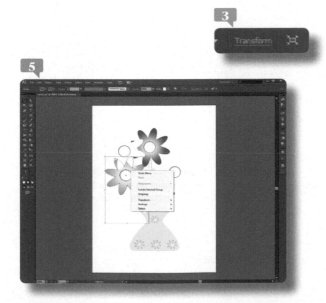

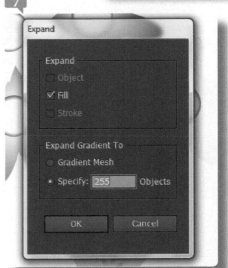

Locking and unlocking objects

ILLUSTRATOR ALLOWS YOU TO LOCK A GROUP of objects or an individual object. By locking objects we prevent them from being modified, either in size, appearance, or position. This option is used when, in a composition, one of the elements should not be changed again. In this exercise you will learn how to lock elements that should not be modified and how to unlock them.

1. You need to work with the file **Vase.ai** again. Then select the vase.

2. Open the **Object** menu and click on the **Lock** command.

3. A submenu with three options opens. The **Selection** option allows you to lock only the selected object in the document. Further, with the help of the second option called **All Artwork Above** you can lock all the objects that are above the selected object and in the same layer, and the last option, **Other Layers,** allows you to lock all layers except the one containing the selected element or group. This time, click on the first option.

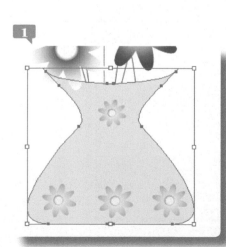

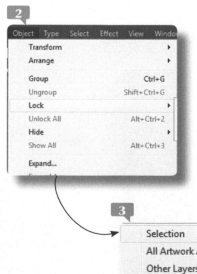

As you can see, it is also possible to lock a selected object by pressing the key combination **Ctrl + 2.**

4. See how the selection of the object has disappeared. In order to verify that it is impossible to select and modify it, click on the vase.

5. Not being able to select the locked object, does it mean you cannot unlock it? No, it does not. The **Object** menu contains an option to delete the locking of all elements in the document. Open this menu and click on the **Unlock All** option.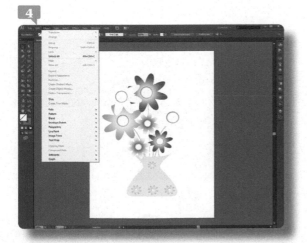

6. Only one object that was locked remains selected, in this case, the star. You will now learn that it is possible to lock and unlock objects from the Layers panel. To display this panel, open the **Window** menu and select the **Layers** option.

7. In your case, the sample document has a single layer that contains all the objects. You can choose to lock the entire layer (and therefore all objects) or display the object list and select the layer you want to lock. In the **Layers** panel, press the white arrow next to the layer name to view the objects it consists of.

8. Click on the gray box next to the eye icon in one of the objects, check if a lock appears on that box, and try to select it.

9. Unlock the object by disabling the lock box and hide the **Layers** panel by pressing the head of the double cursor.

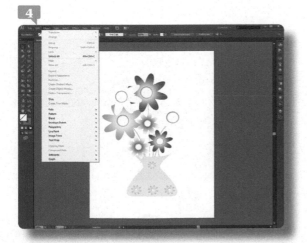

Distributing and aligning objects

THE ALIGNMENT OPTIONS IN ILLUSTRATOR are used to align or distribute selected objects along the specified axis. You can use the edges of objects or anchor points as reference points to align them with a selection, an artboard, or a key object. A key object is one specific object in a selection of multiple objects.

1. Select the central flower at the bottom of the vase and drag it until it is no longer aligned with another flower. 🗨1

2. Select this object and select the objects that will serve as the reference for the alignment. Press the **Shift** key and, without releasing it, click on the two flowers at the bottom of the vase. 🗨2

3. As you know, the **Shift** key is used to make multiple selections. Check if the **Options Bar** displays a link called **Align**, whose keystroke leads you to the panel of the same name. Click on the link in the **Options Bar**. 🗨3

4. The **Align** panel, which contains all alignment and distribution options opens. Your goal is to align the centers of the three flowers and distribute them horizontally. Open the **Align To** command and check if the **Align to Selection** option is enabled. 🗨4

5. Let us have a closer look at the **Align** panel. The first row of

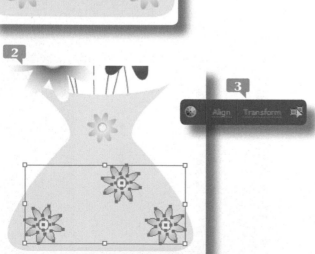

015

options corresponds to the alignment options. You can align objects vertically and horizontally. The icons which represent these options are quite graphic. Click on the fifth icon in the **Align** section that corresponds to the **Vertical Align Center** option. 5

6. The selected objects are aligned vertically with reference to the center. Now distribute them so that the space between them is the same. In the **Align** panel, click on the fifth icon in the **Distribute Objects** section, which corresponds to the **Horizontal Distribute Center** option. 6

7. The objects are distributed correctly. 7 You need to align vertically the small flower of the vase with the flower at the bottom of the vase, this time using the **Align** panel. Click on the small flower, hold down the **Shift** key, and click on the central flower at the bottom of the vase.

8. Open the **Window** menu and select the **Align** option.

9. This opens the **Align** panel. 8 Click on the second icon in the **Align Objects** section that corresponds to the **Horizontal Align Center** option. 9

10. Click on a free area of the document to delete the selection, close the Align panel by clicking on the × button and save the changes by pressing the key combination **Ctrl + S**.

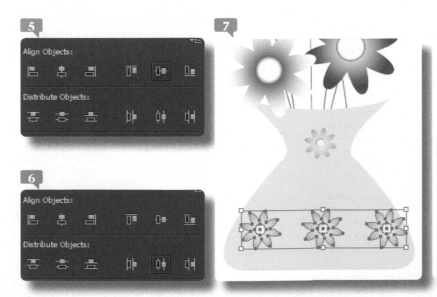

Uniting and combining objects

THE COMBINE COMMAND ALLOWS YOU to merge two or more objects. The lines and colors of the objects are combined to create a new one. As you apply this command, the original objects lose their properties and adopt the features of the first object within all selected images. The parts of the overlapping objects are deleted or cut so you can see what is left.

1. This exercise will show you different ways to combine objects: with the help of compound paths and by using the **Pathfinder** panel effect. If you would like to, you can use the file **Combine.ai**. This file can be found within the download area of our website. Once you have copied the file and opened it in Illustrator, you will start to combine the shapes of the circle and star. Click on the red circle, which acts as a template for the hole. 🔲1

2. Press the **Shift** key and, without releasing it, click on the star below the circle. 🔲2

3. These are the two objects that will combine. Open the **Object** menu and click on the **Compound Path** command. 🔲3

4. Click on the **Make** option, which appears in the submenu, and have a look at the result. 🔲1

5. In fact, the circle's fill has disappeared and reveals the white background of the picture. There is a hole in the middle of the

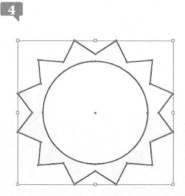

016

circle. You should know that compound paths do not allow a separate manipulation of the objects they consist of. Click on a free area of the document to delete the selection.

6. Continue the exercise by combining the blue ellipses in order to obtain the shape of a cloud. This time you need to use the **Pathfinder** panel. To display this panel, open the **Window** menu and click on the **Pathfinder** option. **5**

7. The **Pathfinder** panel is grouped with the Align panel and the **Transform** panel. Before carrying out any operation, you need to select the shapes you want to combine. Enable the **Selection Tool** in the **Tools** panel and draw by dragging a selection area that covers all the ellipses. **6**

8. In the **Pathfinder** panel, click on the third icon in the **Pathfinder** section that corresponds to the **Merge** option. **7**

9. In order to see the result, click on a free area of the document to delete the selection of the combined group. **8**

10. In the end, you need to combine the two blue circles by using another **Pathfinder** function to obtain the shape of a moon. Select these two shapes **9** and click on the last icon in the **Pathfinder** panel, which corresponds to the **Minus Back** option, **10** and have a look at the result. **11**

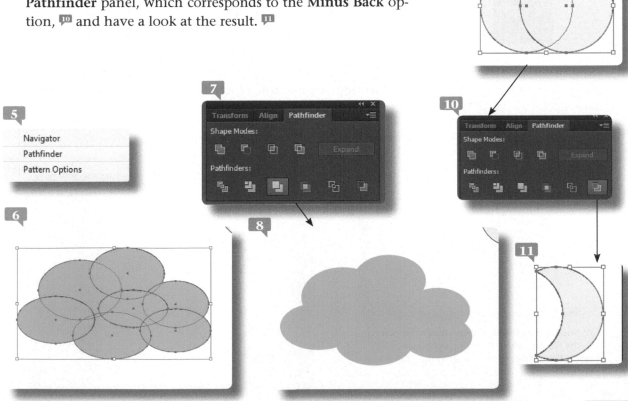

45

Stacking objects

ILLUSTRATOR ORGANIZES SUCCESSIVELY DRAWN objects, beginning with the first object drawn. The order, in which objects are organized, determines how they are displayed when they overlap. The stacking order of objects in your images can be changed at any time.

1. In this exercise, we will show you how to stack the position of drawn objects in a document. In this case, you will just be working with the options of the **Arrange** command. But this change of position is also possible when working with layers (we will discuss this later in the book). You will practice with the document **Combine.ai** again. Change the location of the moon-shaped object (which is created with the help of the combination of two circular shapes). Select and drag the shape of the moon to position it above the cloud by using the **Selection Tool.** [1]

2. The moon is located above the cloud following the order in which the objects were created. (The shape of the moon is positioned above a cloud in the **Layers** panel.) Do you want the moon to be below the cloud? In order to do this, use the **Arrange** command. Open the **Object** menu and click on that command. [2]

As you already know, you can move the objects in the illustration by the drag technique or by using the arrow keys or values in the Transform panel.

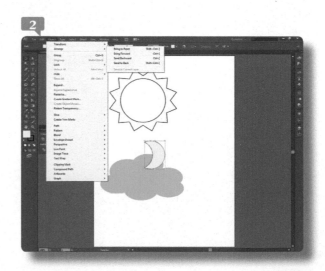

017

3. The **Arrange** command contains five options, whereupon the latter refers to the layers. The **Bring to Front** and **Send to Back** options allow you to place an object in the foreground or background, which is part of the group, whereas the **Bring Forward** and **Send Backward** options allow you to move an object by one object to the front, or one object to the back of the stack. In this case, click on the **Send to Back** option.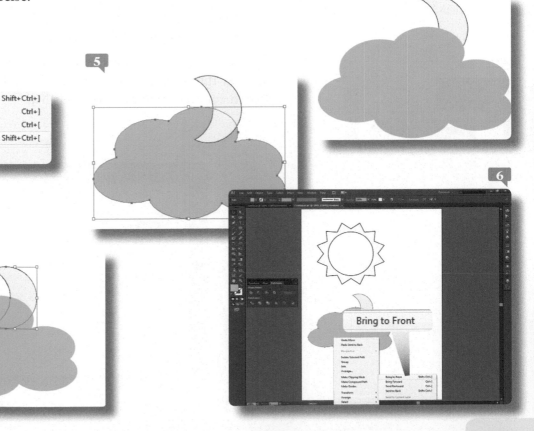

4. Indeed, a part of the moon is hidden under the cloud now. Undo the operation, since we want to show you another way to change the stacking order of objects. Press the key combination **Ctrl + Z** to place the text behind the object.

5. Now you want to perform the reverse operation, that is bring the cloud forward. To do this, click on the figure to select it.

6. Click with the right mouse button on the picture, choose the **Arrange** command within the appearing context menu, and select the **Bring to Front** option.

7. Click on a free area of the document to delete the selection, press the key combination **Ctrl + S** to save the changes and finish the exercise.

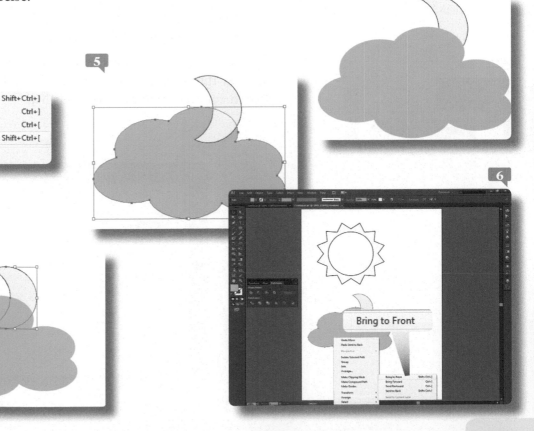

Bring to Front	Shift+Ctrl+]
Bring Forward	Ctrl+]
Send Backward	Ctrl+[
Send to Back	Shift+Ctrl+[
Send to Current Layer	

Creating straight lines

ILLUSTRATOR ALLOWS YOU TO DRAW ALMOST any type of shape. The simplest and most basic shape is the straight line. The program provides the user with the Line Segment Tool, with which it is very easy to draw such lines. In the following exercise, you will learn how to create straight lines in different ways.

1. Open the file named **Project1.ai**, which you have created in a previous lesson, and to which you have applied a colored background. (If you do not have this file any longer, you can download it from our website and copy it to your Documents folder.)

2. As your intention is to draw multiple forms and objects in this document, you need to change its orientation. Click on the **Artboard** icon in the **Tools** panel.

3. In the **Options Bar** of the artboard, click on the **Landscape** command and press the **Esc** key to exit the **Artboard**.

4. As a final document adjustment, open the display field located at the bottom left of the screen and select the **Fit On Screen** command from the options list.

Artboard Tool (Shift+O)

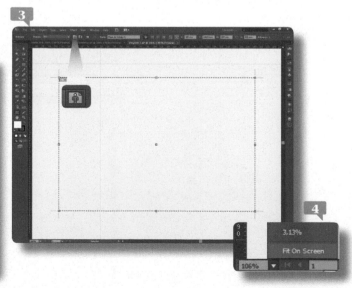

3,13%

Fit On Screen

106%   1

018

5. Start to draw straight lines. Hence, click on the **Line Segment Tool** in the **Tools** panel.

6. Click on the bottom left of the document and, without releasing the mouse button, drag a straight line to the opposite end of the page.

7. Click on the **Selection Tool** and click on a free zone in the document.

8. Draw another line by using another method, but the same tool. Click again on the **Line Segment Tool** in the **Tools** panel.

9. Click on the previously drawn line, approximately at the height of the point 0 on the horizontal ruler.

10. The **Line Segment Tool Options** dialog box opens automatically, in which you need to specify the length and the arc of the shape and if you want to fill it or not. If this option is enabled, the line will be displayed in the current fill color. Click on the **Length** field and enter the value 50.

11. If you would like to specify the angle, you have two options to choose from to do this: enter the exact value in the field to the right or specify it graphically on the image in this table. Type in, for example, the value **90** and press the **OK** button.

12. The line is inserted into the drawing with the specified options. Use the **Selection Tool** to click on a free area to delete the selection and have a look at the result.

Line Segment Tool Options

Length: 50

Angle: 0,05°

Fill Line

OK   Cancel

Angle: 90°

By default, the lines are displayed in blue when they are selected.

Creating rectangles and squares

ILLUSTRATOR PROVIDES THE ESSENTIAL TOOLS to draw basic geometric shapes. Among them, there are tools for rectangles and squares. In this exercise, you will learn how to draw rectangles and squares in Illustrator and how to modify their features. Let's start.

1. Within the **Tools** panel, click on the **Rectangle Tool**, which is located below the **Line Segment Tool**. 🔲

2. In order to draw a rectangle, click on the document, hold down the mouse button, and drag it diagonally down. 🔲

3. In this very simple way you can draw rectangles in your artwork. With the help of the same tool, you will draw a square now. Place the cursor to the right of the rectangle you just drew and when a green line appears from the center of the rectangle, click on it. 🔲

4. Select the **Rectangle Tool** and click on it. Hence, the **Rectangle** dialog box appears, which allows you to specify the dimensions of the figure. Enter the value **25** in the **Width** and **Height** fields and click on **OK** in order to obtain a square. 🔲

Once the shapes are inserted into the illustration, you can edit and modify them by selecting them, and you can change the appropriate values from the panels of the **Options Bar**.

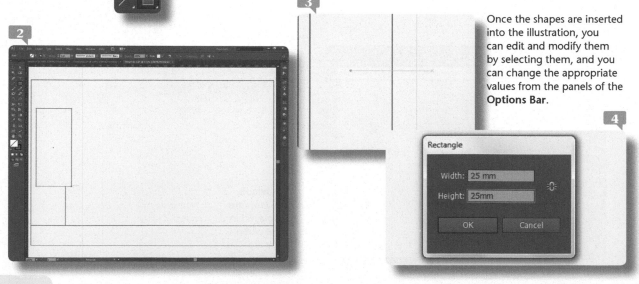

019

5. This is one way to get squares, but there is another way to do this. Select the **Rectangle Tool**, click on the inside of the rectangle, hold down the **Shift** key, and drag diagonally to the right in order to draw another square.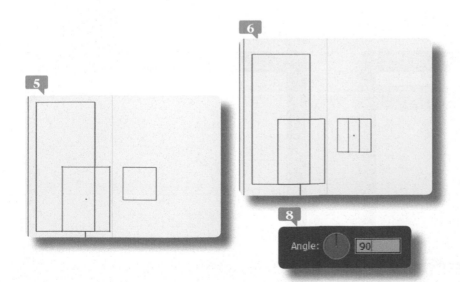

6. As you can see, the **Shift** key helps you to draw squares. Now, you want the three drawn shapes to look like gift boxes. To do this, you need to place small rectangles (which serve as ribbon) on them. On the inside of the smaller square, trace by dragging a rectangle similar to the image.

7. Now you need to duplicate this shape to place it on the other two boxes. Select the **Selection Tool**, hold down the **Alt** key, and drag the shape to the center of the second box (Smart Guides will help you place them easily in the center of the shape).

8. Repeat the action to place the selected shape in the first box, use the handles to increase its height and adjust it to the height of the boxes.

9. You will create a new horizontal rectangle in the small box by using one of the options in the **Object** menu. Open it, click on the **Transform** option and select **Rotate**.

10. In the **Rotate** table, enter the value **90** and press the **Copy** button.

If you follow the steps explained in this exercise, you can complete the images by inserting ribbons on the other boxes and save the changes.

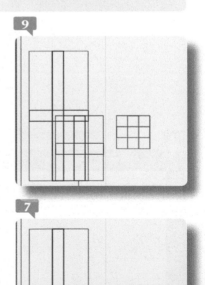

Creating circles and ellipses

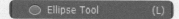
WITH THE HELP OF THE ELLIPSE TOOL you can draw ellipses as well as circles. As for any other shape, once you have drawn it you can resize it through the options in the Options Bar.

1. In this exercise, you will learn how to draw ellipses and circles. The way to do it is in a similar manner to the one seen in the previous exercise on how to draw rectangles and squares. But of course, you need to select the right tool. You will continue to work with the file **Project1.ai**. Go to the **Tools** panel, click on the pointer of the **Rectangle Tool** and select the **Ellipse Tool**. 🔲

2. Click to the right of the box and, without releasing the mouse button, drag diagonally down to create an ellipse. 🔲

3. This is your first ellipse. Duplicate this shape and place it on the other one. To do this, select the **Selection Tool**, click on the ellipse and drag it up by pressing the **Alt** key. 🔲

4. The **Ellipse Tool** also allows you to create perfect circles. This is how you do it. Click again on the tool in the **Tools** panel. 🔲

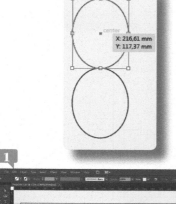

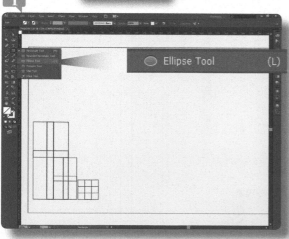

5. Click on the duplicated ellipse, hold down the **Shift** key, and drag it to create a circle that will represent the head of the snowman.

6. In the same way draw three small circles in the ellipse under the circle. The **Duplicate** option can help you to do this and then use the alignment tools in the **Options Bar** to obtain a result similar to the image.

7. There is also another way of drawing ellipses or circles. Select the first ellipse from the bottom and press the **Delete** key to remove it.

8. Select the **Ellipse Tool** again and click at a point under the body of the doll.

9. As you click on it, the **Ellipse** dialog box opens automatically. There, you can specify the dimensions of the figure. To create a circle, you need to enter the same value in the **Width** and **Height** field. In this case, since we want to obtain an ellipse, enter the value **72** for the width and the value **64** for the height and press **OK** to create the figure.

10. You may need to place the new ellipse into the right position. Select it with the adequate tool and use the transformation and alignment controls (which you already learned about) to center it with the other elements of the doll.

11. Complete the drawing by adding eyes to the doll and complete this exercise by deselecting the shapes and saving the changes.

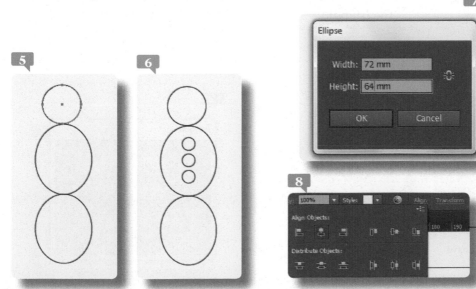

53

Drawing polygons and stars

ILLUSTRATOR ALLOWS YOU TO DRAW EASILY and quickly polygons with different numbers of sides and stars. In both cases, you select the features the figures are supposed to have (such as their form and size).

1. In this exercise, you will work with the **Polygon** and **Star Tools** in order to complete the document **Project1.ai**. Draw a triangle that will serve as the nose of the snowman. Click on the arrow of the **Ellipse Tool** and select the **Polygon Tool**. 🔲

2. In order to have a look at the type of polygon that the tool draws by default, click anywhere on the picture and, without releasing the mouse button, drag it diagonally.

3. As you can see, the default polygon of the program contains six sides. 🔲 Since we want to obtain a triangle, press the **Delete** key to remove the hexagon.

4. Move the pointer to the circle that represents the head of the doll and click on the point where you want to place the nose.

5. In the **Polygon** dialog box, you need to specify the radius of the figure and the number of sides it is supposed to have. In the **Radius** field, enter the value **2** and in the Sides field, type in **3** to indicate the number of sides. Click on **OK** to create the triangle. 🔲

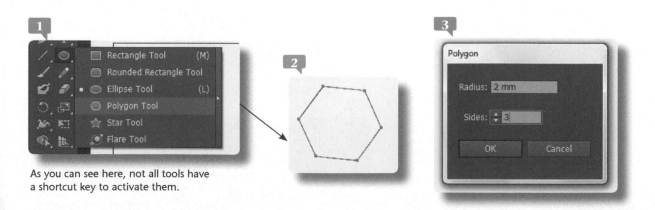

As you can see here, not all tools have a shortcut key to activate them.

021

6. In this case, the figure is a perfect triangle. 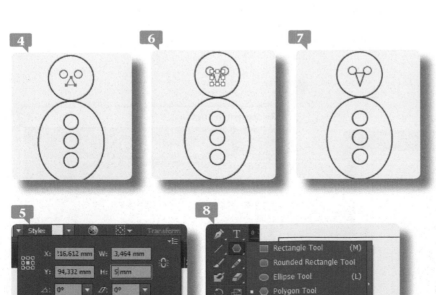 Change the width of the base so that it adapts better to your objects and rotate it. Select the triangle, open the **Transform** panel in the **Options Bar** and enter the value **8** in the **Height** field.

7. You need to use the same **Transform** panel to turn the triangle. Enter the value **180** in the **Rotation Angle** field and press the **Return** key.

8. If the triangle is not in the proper position, you can drag it wherever you want. Once you have placed it, deselect it to have a look at the obtained effect.

9. You will now learn how to draw stars. Open the **Polygon Tool** in the **Tools** panel, and select the **Star Tool** from the list.

10. By dragging, draw several stars with different sizes at the bottom of the figure and the body of the snowman.

11. As you can see, by default, the stars drawn by Illustrator have 5 points. You can modify this feature according to your preferences. Select the **Star Tool** and click on a free area in the illustration.

12. Enter the value **7** in the **Points** field of the **Star** dialog box and click on **OK** to create a new star.

IMPORTANT

In the **Star** dialog box you can specify three values: **Radius 1** with which you can indicate the distance from the center of the star to the most inner points, **Radius 2** to establish the distance from the center of the star to the outermost points, and points which help you to specify the number of points the star should have.

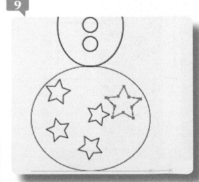

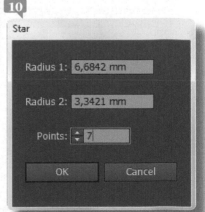

Drawing arcs

IN THE SAME GROUP where you find the Line Segment Tool, Illustrator provides the user with a tool that can create arcs: the Arc Tool.

1. Draw an arc in the **Project1.ai** document, which will serve as the mouth of the snowman. To work in greater detail, expand the display of the drawing. Open the field at the bottom left of the window, and select a value of **200%**. 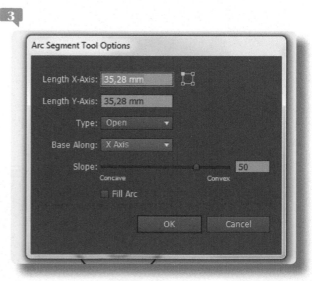 Use the scroll bars to center the head of the snowman in the work area.

2. In the **Tools** panel, click on the arrow of the **Line Segment Tool** and select the **Arc Tool**.

3. As with the other drawing tools you have worked with so far, the technique to draw arcs is by dragging. But since you want to obtain a specific shape, a smile, you need to display the options of the arc first. Click on an area of the head where you want to place the mouth.

4. This opens the **Arc Segment Tool Options** dialog box. The length of the X-axis corresponds to the amplitude of the arc in question. In this case, enter the value **5** in this field.

022

5. Of course, the length of the Y-axis corresponds to the height of the arc. In order to obtain a proportional arc, you also need to enter the value **5** in this field.

6. The **Type** field allows you to specify if the path is supposed to be open (which is the selected default option) or closed. If it is closed, the result will be similar to a part of a circular object. Keep the default option. The next field, called **Base Along**, specifies the direction of the arc, which can be either horizontal or vertical. By default, the selected option is X, which means horizontal. Click on the arrow of that field and select **Y-Axis**.

7. You can also change the slope value of the arc. This value indicates the direction of the arc's slope: a negative value will create a concave (inward) slope, while a positive value will create a convex (outward) slope. Enter the value **40** in this field and press **OK** to create the arc.

8. The arc is inserted into the area of the image you clicked on previously. You can change its location and slope. For the latter, select the **Rotate Tool** in the **Tools** panel, click on the right end of the arc and drag it until you obtain the desired angle.

9. Use the **Selection Tool** to move the arc to your preferred area and click on a free zone to have a look at the final result.

IMPORTANT

If you want to see a dynamic preview of the arc as you set its options, open it by double-clicking on the Arc Tool.

4
Length X-Axis: 5 mm
Length Y-Axis: 5 mm

5
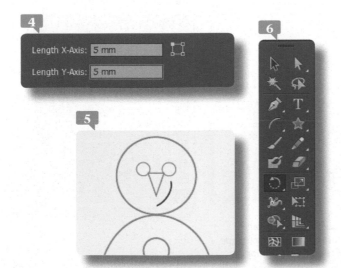

6

7
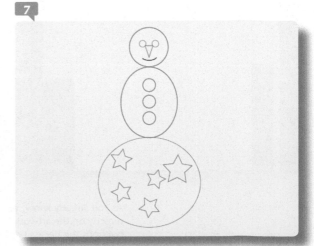

Drawing spirals

THE SPIRAL TOOL DRAWS SPIRALS in two ways. In the Tools panel, this tool is grouped within the Line Segment, Arc, and Grid Tools and is applied by using the drag technique.

1. Before you start practicing with the **Spiral Tool**, you need to reduce the zoom of the **Project1.ai** document from the previous exercise. To do this, open the display field, which is located at the bottom left of the workspace, and select the option **Fit On Screen** as it appears in the drop-down menu. 🔲

2. Click on the pointer of the **Arc Tool** and click on the **Spiral Tool**. 🔲

3. Create two facing and united spirals that will represent the loop of one of the gifts. Click on the smaller box.

4. Within the appearing **Spiral** dialog box you can find various preset values. The first corresponds to the radius of the figure. Modify this parameter by entering the value **7** in the **Radius** field. 🔲

5. In the next field, called **Decay**, you can establish the degree to which each wind of the spiral should decrease relative to

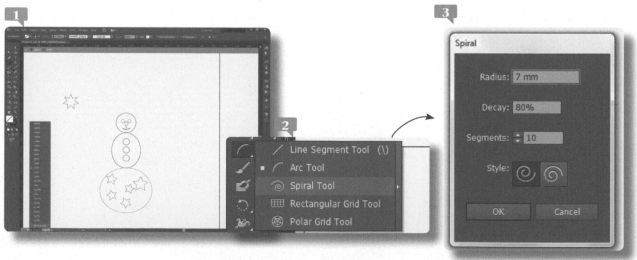

As you already know, you can draw the spiral directly on the artwork by using the drag technique (without the necessity of displaying the options).

the previous wind. You will keep the default percentage of 80%. In addition, the **Segments** field specifies the number of segments the spiral has. Each wind of the spiral consists of 4 segments. In this case, you will neither change the value nor the style of the spiral, so you can press the **OK** button in order to create the first spiral.

6. The spiral is placed into the area you have previously chosen. If necessary, you can move it with the **Selection Tool** and place it into the right position. For the second spiral use the same values, but change the style. Select the **Spiral Tool** and click on the right end of the figure you just drew.

7. In the **Spiral** dialog box, click on the Options button of the second style and press **OK**.

8. The center of the new spiral is placed into the area you have indicated. You need to use a transformation command that will allow you to turn the new spiral as if it was a reflection. Thus, your main interest is the orientation. Right-click on the new spiral, then on the **Transform** command (which is displayed in the context menu) and select the **Reflect** option.

9. The object rotates while the **Reflection** option box opens automatically. Press **OK** to maintain these options and have a look at the result.

10. Now you just need to place the spiral correctly. Use the **Select** and **Rotate tools** to position it as in the image.

> ## IMPORTANT
>
> The **Reflect Tool** reflects the objects over a fixed axis. This command can be found in the Tools panel and can also be activated from the context menu of the object or from the **Transform** submenu in the **Object** menu.
>
>

The **Style** field allows you to specify the direction of the spiral.

If you want to change the location, orientation, or any other feature of the two spirals at the same time, group them together.

Drawing grids

THE ILLUSTRATOR GRID TOOLS allow you to quickly and easily draw grids such as rectangles, polar grids, or circles.

1. In this exercise, you will use the **Rectangular Grid** Tool to draw a windmill in our sample document **Project1.ai**. Click on the pointer of the **Spiral Tool** and select the **Rectangular Grid Tool** within the tools list of the group.

2. Once you have selected the tool, you can proceed in two ways: by clicking and dragging on the work area or by displaying the Options box of the tool to configure it as done previously. In this case, click on the vertical line that you drew in a previous exercise, and, without releasing the mouse button, drag it diagonally to the left to obtain a result similar to the image.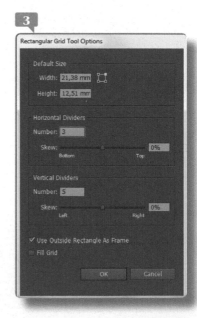

3. The grid is drawn with a number of horizontal and vertical predetermined dividers, specifically five. These parameters can be changed from the Options box of this tool. To do this, press the key combination **Ctrl + Z** to undo the drawing of the grid. Then keep the tool in the **Tools** panel selected and click on the same point as before.

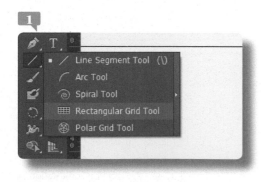

You can preset the dimensions of the grid in the Options box of the tool.

4. In the **Rectangular Grid Tool Options** box, enter the value **3** in the **Number** field of the **Horizontal Dividers** section. [3]

5. The **Skew** value determines how the horizontal dividers are weighted toward the top or bottom of the grid. In this case, enter the value **18** in the **Skew** field of the same section and press the **OK** button. [4]

6. Now the lower rows of the grid are higher than the upper ones. [5] Change the angle of inclination of the grid and create multiple copies to obtain the desired result. With the help of the **Selection Tool**, select the grid. Move the cursor close to one of its corners and as it changes into the shape of a curved arrow, drag the grid slightly to incline it. [6]

7. Click with the right mouse button on the grid, click on the **Transform** option and select **Reflect**.

8. Enable the **Vertical** option in the **Reflect** table [7] and press the **Copy** button. Drag the copy of the grid to place it correctly and repeat it twice more to obtain a result similar to the image. [8]

IMPORTANT

The Options box of the **Polar Grid Tool** contains the same options as the Rectangular Grid Tool, although the terminology has been adapted to the type of resulting figure. So instead of Horizontal dividers, the Polar Grid has concentric dividers, and the vertical dividers are called radial dividers.

> Concentric Dividers
>
> Number: 5

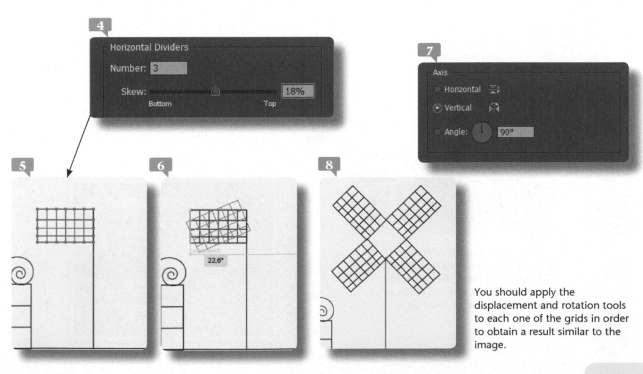

You should apply the displacement and rotation tools to each one of the grids in order to obtain a result similar to the image.

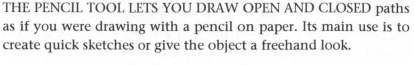

Drawing with the Pencil Tool

THE PENCIL TOOL LETS YOU DRAW OPEN AND CLOSED paths as if you were drawing with a pencil on paper. Its main use is to create quick sketches or give the object a freehand look.

IMPORTANT

As you draw with the **Pencil Tool**, anchor points are randomly created, which you can adjust after completing the path. The number of created anchor points is determined by the length and complexity of the path and by the Tolerance settings of the Options dialog box of the tool.

1. In this exercise, you will work with the **Pencil Tool**. However, before drawing new elements, you need to create a new layer in the illustration **Project1.ai**. Layers help you to manage the elements of the image more easily, since they allow you to modify these elements individually and independently of other objects. To create a new layer, click on the next to last icon in the collapsed panels list to the right. 🔲

2. As you can see in the **Layers** panel, all elements drawn until this moment are placed in one layer, called **Layer 1**. Click on the third icon called **Create new layer** in the row of icons at the bottom of the panel. 🔲

3. The new layer is placed on the original one. Double-click on the name **Layer 2**, write in the **Name** field of the **Layers Options** dialog box the name **Pencil** and press the **OK** button to confirm. 🔲

4. You already have the new layer, where you will place the elements drawn with the **Pencil Tool**. In the **Tools** panel, click on this command. 🔲

The key that activates the **Pencil Tool** is **L**.

In addition to working with layers, it is highly recommended that you work with artboards, since they allow you to create different versions of the same image and to arrange them all on screen.

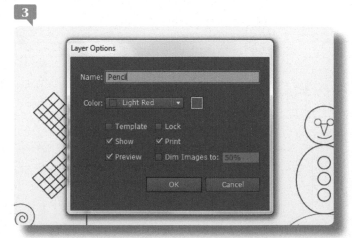

5. Your goal is to achieve a type of loop for some of the ribbons on the gifts. The **Pencil Tool** uses the drag technique as the drawing method: as if it were drawn on paper. Click on one of the boxes, press the **Alt** key and, without releasing the mouse button, drag the pointer to the desired shape.

6. You can create closed paths if you press the **Alt** key while drawing. If you do not press this key, you can obtain simple or open paths. In general, the path with the drawing tools requires certain abilities in handling the mouse, since the results will be more or less spectacular depending on your skills. Select the **Pencil Tool** and by double-clicking on it in the **Tools** panel, access the Options box.

7. The **Pencil Tool Options** dialog box opens. The **Fidelity** and **Smoothness** options will appear in the **Tolerances** section. The Fidelity option controls the distance you need to move the mouse to add a new anchor point to the path, whereas the Smoothness option controls the amount of smoothness that is applied to use this tool. Keep the options as they appear by default and click on **Cancel** to exit this box.

8. Click on the **Selection Tool** in the **Tools** panel and click on a free area of the illustration to have a better look at the result.

IMPORTANT

The color applied to the layers of a document is reflected as you select the drawn objects in them. So, if you have applied the color red to the layer Pencil, it changes into red as you select the created drawing in this layer. Another issue is the color of the stroke, which is defined by the stroke sample selected in the Tools panel.

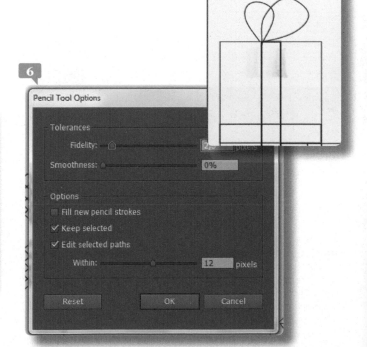

If you have used the **Alt** key to create a closed path, it is not necessary to place the mouse cursor over the starting point of the drawing to close it.

Drawing with the Pen Tool

THE PEN TOOL IN ILLUSTRATOR IS USED TO DRAW straight lines and curves to create customized objects. This tool is implementated with the help of clicks, adding an anchor point for each click.

1. In this exercise, we will show you how to use the **Pen Tool** in Illustrator. To do this, you will create two types of paths in your **Project1.ai** document: a straight and a curved one. Place the new drawing in a new layer. In the **Layers** panel, click on the **New Layer** icon. 1

2. Rename the new layer as **Pen** and press **Return** to confirm the name and activate it. 2

3. Select the **Pen Tool** (which is displayed by the tip of a pen) in the **Tools** panel. 3

4. As you select the **Pen Tool**, the mouse changes into a new shape accompanied by a plus (+) sign. This indicates that you can begin to add anchor points. The first path will be straight. Click to the right of the snowman, at the height of the head, to place on this point the first anchor point. 4

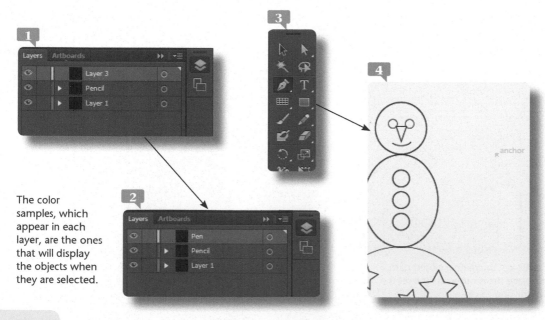

The color samples, which appear in each layer, are the ones that will display the objects when they are selected.

The first anchor point appears as a small solid square, which changes into a hole by introducing the next anchor point.

64

5. Enter the second point of the straight segment by clicking a few inches to the right. **5**

6. Enter three anchor points by clicking on the document and close the path by clicking on the first anchor point to obtain a result similar to the image. **6**

7. In order to disable the tool, press the **Ctrl** key and click on a free area of the illustration.

8. As we have said before, the **Pen Tool** allows you to create curved paths. Now you will see how. Select the new tool, click on the bottom left of the path you have just created and drag it an inch upward. **7**

9. At each end of the line handles have appeared that allow you to distort these lines until you obtain a curved path. To do this, click on the upper end of the segment, hold down the mouse button, and drag it up or down depending on the angle you want to apply to the path. **8**

10. According to your preferences, you can also stretch it to the right, left, or diagonally. You can place as many anchor points as you like, but please know that if you use too many points, you can cause unwanted distortions in the curves. Press the **Ctrl** key and click on a free area of the image to have a look at the final result. **9**

026

IMPORTANT

You should know that the first anchor point is not displayed until the second one is determined. Moreover, as you finish the path you can close it or leave it open. In order to close it you need to click on the first inserted anchor point, and if you want to keep it open, you need to press the Ctrl key and click on a free area of the workspace.

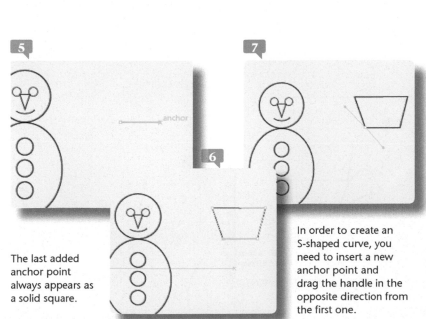

The last added anchor point always appears as a solid square.

In order to create an S-shaped curve, you need to insert a new anchor point and drag the handle in the opposite direction from the first one.

Editing anchor points

ANY STRAIGHT OR CURVED PATH CREATED with the Pen Tool consists of anchor points and can be modified in various ways.

1. In this exercise, you will learn how to edit paths that you created with the **Pen Tool** in the previous exercise. There are different ways to select the anchor points of a path. In the **Tools** panel, click on the **Direct Selection Tool,** which is displayed by a white arrow.

2. Click on the bottom right anchor point of the straight path, which was created by the **Pen Tool.**

3. After selecting the anchor point, you can modify its position. To do this, click again on the anchor point, hold down the mouse button, and drag the segment until it changes its shape.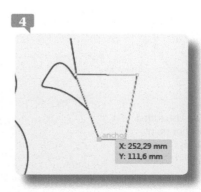

4. Keep the **Direct Selection Tool** active, click on one of the anchor points of the path and drag it until it distorts.

5. Press the **Ctrl** key and click on a free area of the image.

6. Another way to edit paths created with the **Pen Tool** is to select the segments that they are made of. To do this, you need

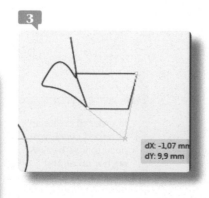

to use the **Direct Selection Tool**. Select this tool, and click on one of the drawing's segments.

7. See how the whole figure is selected by clicking on one of the path segments. This means that you can modify it as a whole. In this case, change the location to place it above and slightly modify the inclination. Click on it and drag it slightly upward. 5

8. Select the **Rotate Tool** in the **Tools** panel, click on the top right anchor point of the path with which you are practicing and, without releasing the mouse button, drag it to change the inclination. 6

9. Modify the look of the open path (the ones you have drawn in the precious exercise) according to your preferences with the help of the **Free Selection**, **Selection**, and **Rotate** Tools. 7

10. If you are finished with the modification, click on a free area of the illustration while holding down the **Ctrl** key to have a look at the result. 8

027

IMPORTANT

In order to select several individual anchor points at once, you can either decide to press the **Shift** key while selecting them or use the Lasso Tool to mark the area that you want to select.

By moving and turning the different anchor points of a path drawn by the Pen Tool, you can completely change the appearance of the object.

Converting lines to curves and vice versa

THE CONVERT ANCHOR POINT TOOL IS THE MOST accurate way to perform a conversion from a straight line to a curved one and vice versa. However, such a conversion can also be carried out thanks to the Smooth function.

1. In the following exercise, you will learn how to convert the vertices of a straight path into one with curves, and also how to obtain the opposite effect. Before converting the vertices of the closed path with the **Pen Tool** (the ones you created in a previous exercise) so you get a more rounded figure, you need to delete one of the existing anchor points. You can copy the **Project2.ai** file, from the download area of our website if you want to work with an updated version of the sample file that you are creating. Click on the pointer of the **Pen Tool** and select the **Delete Anchor Point** tool.

2. As you place the mouse cursor over a path, Illustrator will inform you about the path's anchor points. For example, click on the lower right anchor point of the closed shape that was created by the **Pen Tool**, and have a look at the new shape that results from the disappearance of the anchor point.

3. Click on the second icon in the **Convert** section of the **Options Bar**, which is called **Convert selected anchor points to smooth**.

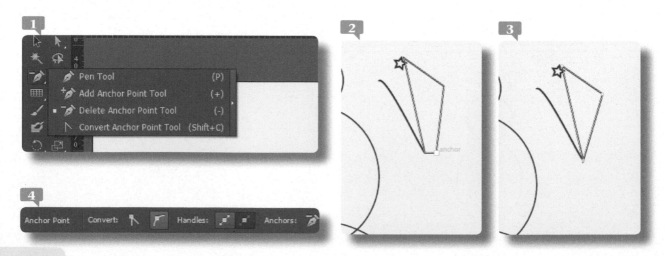

4. See how the selected anchor point converted into a curved one, displaying the handles that allow you to edit it. **5** If you need to change another anchor point, select the **Direct Selection Tool 6** and press the same command.

5. Press the **Ctrl** key and click on a free area of the illustration to have a better look at the result. **7**

6. To obtain the opposite effect, that is to convert the curves of a path into straight vertices, you need to do the same. Draw a curve similar to the image with the **Pen Tool. 8**

7. Click on the path to select it with the **Direct Selection Tool.**

8. Click on the anchor point you want to smooth and in the **Options Bar**, click on the **Convert selected anchor points to corner** icon. **9**

9. In this case, since it is a very simple path, convert the curved line into a simple straight segment. Working with anchor points requires certain skills and dexterity, so we recommend you get to know the possibilities of these drawing elements on you own. To finish this exercise, click on any free area of the artboard to deselect the path and save the changes by pressing the key combination **Ctrl + S. 10**

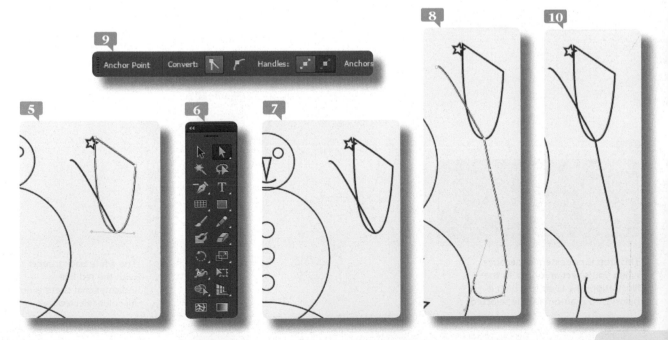

Adding a fill to an object

A COLOR OR GRADIENT APPLIED TO THE INNER AREA of an open or closed path is called a fill. By default, all closed paths drawn in Illustrator display no fill. However, thanks to the extensive color palette of the program, you can apply any fill color.

1. In this exercise, you will start working with colors in the **Project2.ai** file. In this case, you will use the **Color Picker**, which is accessible from the **Tools** panel, the **Eyedropper Tool** and the **Color** panel. Let's start by applying a fill to our figure, the snowman. To do this, in the **Layers** palette, select **Layer 1,** which is the layer where the figure is located. **1**

2. Click on the circular shape that serves as the head of the snowman, then by holding down the **Shift** key, select the other two shapes that represent the body so you can apply the same color to the selected parts all at once. **2**

3. Double-click on the fill color swatch in the Tools panel, which displays a white background under a diagonal red line. **3**

4. If you double-click on one part of the document, the **Color picker** dialog box opens, and if you click on another part, the

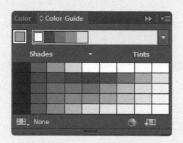

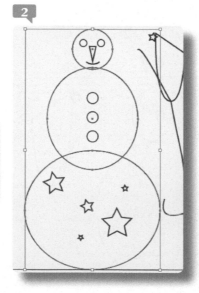

This step is not essential because when you select an object in the illustration, the layer to which it belongs to is automatically selected.

The white background with the red line indicates that there is no fill color selected.

029

Color panel is displayed. Be aware of the fact that the **Color Picker** can be opened from these two elements. In the bar that displays the range of colors, click on the blue tones and select a light hue in the spectrum on the left. Click on **OK** to apply the color to the selected objects. 🗨

5. See how, apart from coloring the selected objects, the chosen swatch now appears in the **Tools** panel both in the **Color** panel and in the **Options Bar.** 🗨 Remember that the applied background of the previous exercises affects the display of the applied colors. If you want to remove this background, access the **Document Setup** box and disable the **Simulate Paper Color** option. In Illustrator, the **Eyedropper Tool** also allows you to apply a fill. This tool applies the current attributes, among which you can find the Fill and Stroke. In the **Tools** panel, click on the **Eyedropper Tool,** which precisely displays this object. 🗨

6. Press the **Alt** key and, without releasing it, click on the stars drawn outside of the snowman to fill them with the sampled color. 🗨

7. It is very easy to apply the current fill color. Click on a zone free of the artwork to deselect the objects and save the changes to the document by pressing the key combination **Ctrl + S**.

Varying the stroke characteristics

A STROKE CAN BE THE VISIBLE OUTLINE OF AN OBJECT, a path, or the edge of a Live Paint group. By default, Illustrator draws the lines in black and with a continuous thin line, but you can change these characteristics according to your needs and preferences.

1. In this exercise you will learn how to apply a stroke color other than the default one and how to modify the width of this element by using the new Variable Width function. You will work on one of the previously drawn stars in your illustration from the previous exercises. Use the **Selection Tool** to click on one of these figures. 📑

2. In the **Options Bar**, click on the pointer of the **Stroke** button, which is shown as a black outline. 📑

3. The **Swatches** panel opens. Click on one of the dark blue swatches 📑 and click on a free area in the artwork in order to have a look at the color applied to the stroke. 📑

4. The stroke of the star displays the selected blue color. Apply a fill color to the star from the **Options Bar**. Reselect the star.

5. Open the **Fill** button in the **Options Bar**, which can be found to the left of the **Stroke** button, choose a silvery gray tone 📑

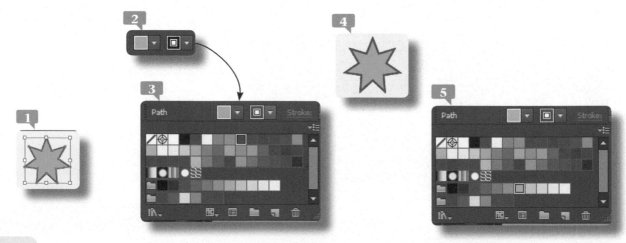

and click on a free area of the illustration to deselect it and have a look at the result.

6. You will increase the width of the stroke of this star by using the new **Width Tool**, with which it is possible to create lines of different width and store the variable width as a profile that can then be applied to other strokes. After selecting the star again, increase the zoom display, and click on the **Width Tool** which is the second icon in the third group in the **Tools** panel.

7. As you place the mouse cursor over the stroke that makes up the shape, a diamond appears on the path, which you can drag to increase or decrease the width in certain parts of the path. Click on one of the points of the star, drag it into the shape and see how it reduces the width of the stroke. Repeat it with the other side by dragging it outward this time.

8. You can also create or edit a width point using the **Width Point Edit** dialog box. Open it by double-clicking on a star tip with the **Width Tool**, set a width of **0.5 mm** for side **1** and **0.7 mm** for side **2** and apply the effect by pressing **OK**.

9. This way you can edit the width of each stroke to obtain different shapes. Practice on your own with this tool and, when the star is sufficiently modified, deselect it and save the changes.

IMPORTANT

Besides the color and the width of the stroke, Illustrator also lets you change the **shape of the stroke**, which is by default **Basic**, that is, continuous.

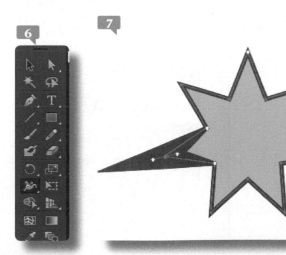

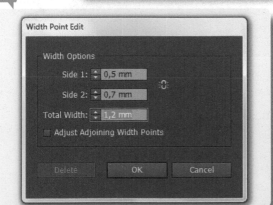

Selecting and deleting fills and strokes

ILLUSTRATOR CONTAINS THE NECESSARY COMMANDS and tools to remove strokes and fills applied to an object.

1. In this exercise, you will learn how to delete an object's fill and stroke. You will also get to know a really useful function that allows you to select objects that display the same fill and stroke attributes. Begin with this function. Enable the **Selection Tool** and click on one of the stars that displays the fill color as blue.

2. Locate the objects that have the same fill. To do this, go to the **Options Bar**, click on the pointer that goes with the **Select Similar Objects** button in the menu that appears, and then click on the **Fill Color** option.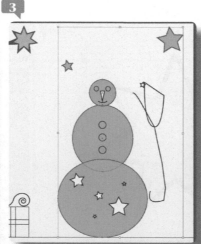

3. All objects with the same fill color are immediately selected. In this case, remove the fill color. 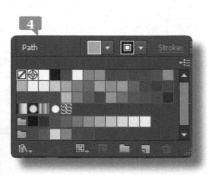 Press the Shift key and clear the central element that represents the body of the snowman. Then, in the **Options Bar**, open the **Fill** field and click on the first swatch in the **Swatch** palette, which is called **No Fill**.

031

4. The Fill color of the selected objects is deleted instantly. Apart from using the **Swatches** panel of the Options Bar, you can also remove the fill color from the **Tools** panel. Now you are going to look at the stroke that was used on the figures. Deselect the selected shapes and select only those stars that have no fill color.

5. Use the **Fill** control of the **Options Bar** to apply a clear blue to them.

6. Change the stroke of these stars. In this case, display the **Stroke Weight** field and choose a slightly larger size than the current one.

7. It is possible to remove the stroke of an object, while keeping the fill only. Deselect the stars, whose stroke weight you just modified, and select just one of the stars.

8. In the **Options Bar**, click the **Stroke** color field and in the **Swatch** panel, click on the first swatch that corresponds to the color **None**.

9. Click on a free area in the artwork to deselect the star, have a look at the result to finish the exercise.

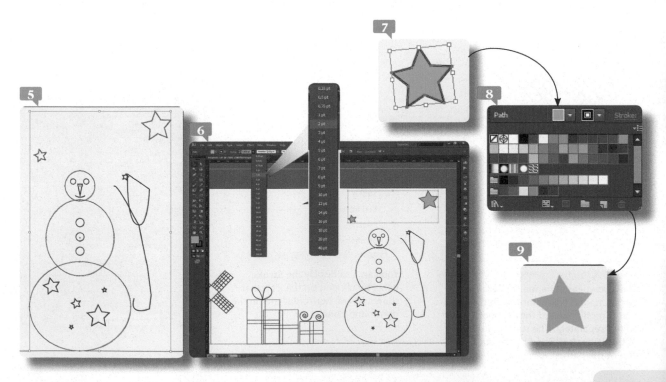

Inserting and customizing arrowheads

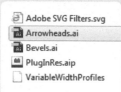
ILLUSTRATOR ENABLES THE USER TO TAKE ADVANTAGE of an extensive catalog of arrowheads to convert simple lines (straight or curved ones) into arrows. In Illustrator CS6 arrowheads are not inserted as effects but they are added from the Stroke panel.

1. In this exercise, you will learn how to turn a simple straight line into an arrow. To do this, you will use the arrowhead effects provided by Illustrator. You will work on the straight line below the blades in the **Project2.ai** document. Enable the **Selection Tool** and click on the previously mentioned line. 🔲

2. You should know that you cannot apply arrowheads to individual paths that are part of a Live Paint group (we will talk about these groups later in this book). Open the **Stroke** panel by selecting it from the **Window** menu. 🔲

3. In this version of Illustrator CS6, as you can see, the **Stroke** panel contains a section called **Arrowheads**. 🔲 You can access this section by displaying the options where you can add arrowheads from the start to the end point of a drawing. To

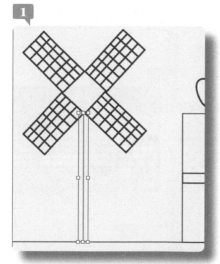

The arrowheads change the location, direction, and color along with the line that is modified, and they cannot be edited separately. The start and the end of the arrow is defined by the start and end of the path.

You can also display the **Stroke** panel by clicking on the icon that shows several horizontal lines in the right-hand panel.

display the Arrowheads gallery, click on the button of the first field next to the **Arrowheads** section.

4. Scroll through the Arrowheads gallery with the help of the vertical scroll bar and select the design you prefer most. 4

5. Repeat the process to select a design for the end of the line. 5

6. Note that you can choose different designs for the two ends of the line. The **Scale** field in this section is used to change the size of the arrowheads. If you want the scale to be the same for both ends, you need to enable the Chain icon, which appears on the right. For example, reduce the scale of the first arrowhead by **80%** 6 and have a look at the effect. 7

7. In order to remove arrowheads from the paths, you need to select the **None** option in this panel. Once you have created the arrowheads, you can modify them in different ways, one of which is to change its features from the **Appearance** panel. With the line selected, open that panel from the **Window** menu.

8. To change the line color, open the **Swatches** panel of the **Stroke** field and select a color you like. 8

9. Deselect the line and save the changes to your drawing by pressing the key combination **Ctrl + S**.

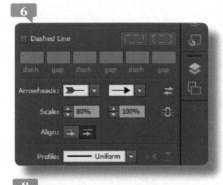

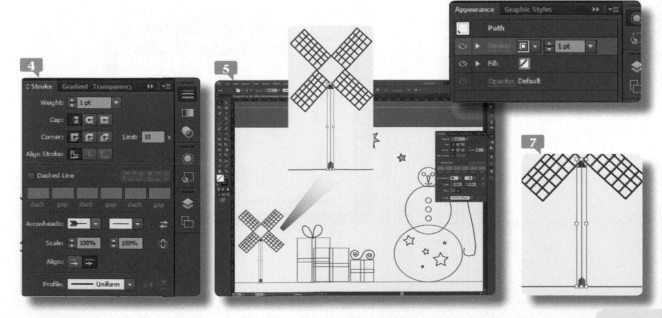

Dividing, cutting, and trimming objects

ILLUSTRATOR PROVIDES SEVERAL WAYS TO DIVIDE, cut, and trim objects. Each method can be used according to the changes you want to make in the illustration.

1. In this exercise you will learn only some of the functions and commands since there are many that allow you to perform these actions. Begin with the **Divide Objects Below** command, which uses an object as a template to cut other objects. Click on one of the stars in the drawing to select it as a template.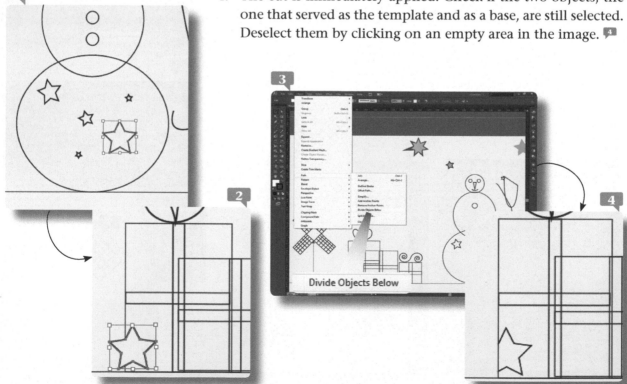

2. Click on the star again and drag it to overlap it with one of the gift boxes.

3. Open the **Object** menu, click on the **Path** command and select the **Divide Objects Below** option in the submenu that appears.

4. The cut is immediately applied. Check if the two objects, the one that served as the template and as a base, are still selected. Deselect them by clicking on an empty area in the image.

Divide Objects Below

033

5. Now you will learn another method of cutting and dividing objects. This time, you will use the **Knife Tool**, which cuts objects along a freehand path you will draw, dividing objects into their components. In the **Tools** panel, click on the **Eraser Tool** (which displays a picture of an eraser) and in the appearing panel, select the **Knife Tool**. [5]

6. To draw a freehand straight line that divides one of the stars, hold down the **Alt** key and drag the pointer to that object. [6]

7. As you release the mouse button, the divided object remains selected. Now you can work on any of its parts. Activate the **Selection Tool**, deselect the object, select only one of its parts, and repeatedly press the key combination **Shift + the left arrow key** to separate it from the other. [7]

8. Click on a free area in the artwork to remove the selection of the object and have a look at the result. [8]

9. A final method used to cut and divide objects is the **Scissors Tool**, which can only be applied to paths that use anchor points. Click on the pointer of the **Knife Tool** in the **Tools** panel and select the **Scissors Tool**. [9]

10. Click on the curved line next to the snowman and repeatedly press the Shift and direction key to the left to divide one part from the other. [10]

11. Click with the **Selection Tool** on a free area within the illustration to deselect the path and save the changes.

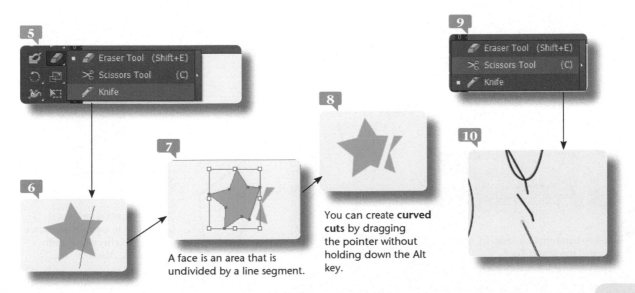

A face is an area that is undivided by a line segment.

You can create **curved cuts** by dragging the pointer without holding down the Alt key.

Erasing paths with the Eraser Tool

ILLUSTRATOR CONTAINS THE PATH ERASER TOOL, the Eraser Tool, or the eraser of a Wacom stylus pen that lets you eliminate parts of an illustration.

1. In this exercise, you will learn how to remove a part of a path with the **Eraser Tool**. Simply click on the pointer of the **Scissors Tool**, the last one selected in the **Tools** panel of the previous exercise, and select the panel that displays the **Eraser Tool**. 🔲

2. The mouse pointer now changes into a target. Using this tool is really simple: you need to slide the pointer over the object you want to delete. Try it out. Click on a part of the separate line from the previous exercise. 🔲

3. As you can see, the part of the path you clicked on has now disappeared. Erase the little star next to the line fragment you just deleted in the same way. You can see the default characteristics (diameter, roundness, etc.) of the **Eraser Tool** as you also remove a part of the path next to this star and release the mouse button. 🔲

4. The **Eraser Tool** has a complete table of options to change various parameters such as diameter, angle, or the roundness

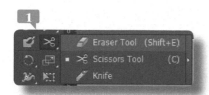

The key combination Shift + E also activates the Eraser Tool.

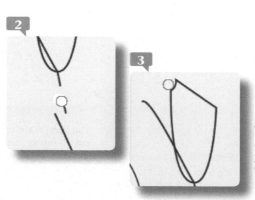

When the Eraser Tool is applied to parts of an object, you can check their path features, diameter, etc.

of the draft. To access this option box, double-click on the command in the **Tools** panel. 4

5. In this case, only change the diameter of the easer. To do this, double-click on the **Size** field and enter the value **12 pt**. 5

6. The pop-up list to the right of each option allows you to control the variations of the shape of the tool. The available options are **Fixed** (active by default) and **Random** (within a preset range). The other options (**Pressure**, **Stylus Wheel**, **Tilt**, **Direction**, and **Rotation**) are only applicable when you are using an electronic pen as a drawing instrument. In this case, you will keep the **Fixed** option selected. Press the **OK** button to apply the new parameter.

7. Increasing the diameter of the tool will allow you to remove larger areas of the picture more quickly. As an example, delete some parts of the star (which got divided in a previous exercise) by using the drag technique. 6

8. The part drawn with the **Eraser Tool** has disappeared from the picture. 7 Another way to remove complete paths is, as discussed in a previous exercised, to use the **Delete** key after selecting the object you want to delete. Click on the **Selection Tool** in the **Tools** panel and click on one of the stars drawn on the body of the snowman. 8

9. Press the **Delete** key on your keyboard to delete the selected object 9 and save the changes by pressing the key combination **Ctrl + S**.

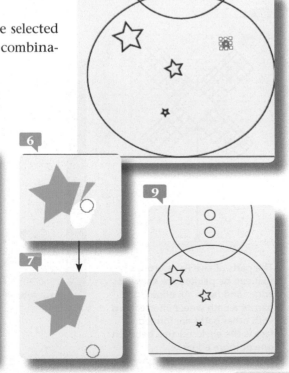

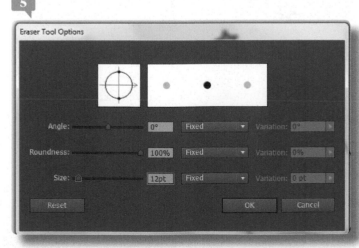

Creating a Live Paint group

ILLUSTRATOR OFFERS TWO PAINTING METHODS: assign a fill, stroke, or both to an entire object, or convert the object into a Live Paint group and assign fills or strokes to different edges and faces of the paths.

1. In this first exercise, you will learn how to create one of these painting groups from an already created object. To do this, you will work on rectangular grids drawn on the bottom left part of the **Project2.ai** file. Select one of these grids with the **Selection** tool.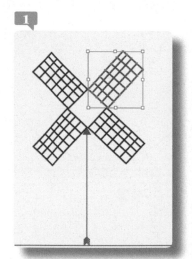

2. Objects, which can be converted into Live Paint groups, can be traced or compound paths. Open the **Object** menu and click on the **Live Paint** command.

3. In the submenu that appears select the **Create** option.

4. Although it seems that nothing has happened, the Options Bar confirms that the selected object has been converted into a Live Paint group. This means that all the parts of the grid and all paths can be colored with different colors. You'll prac-

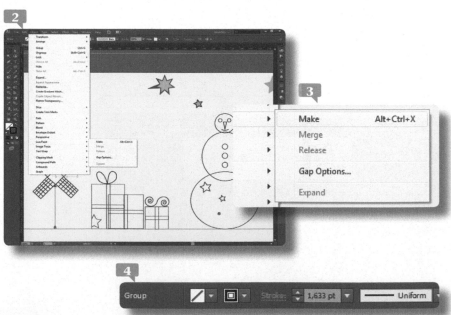

The parts of Live Paint groups that can be painted are known as edges and faces. An edge is the part of a path where intersections with other paths are formed. A face is the enclosed area between one or more edges.

Group / ▾ | ▾ Stroke: 1,633 pt ▾ ——— Uniform

tice this action in the following exercise. To select the parts that form a Live Paint group, Illustrator has a selection tool for these groups, but you can also use the conventional Selection Tool if you want to fill the Live Paint group with the same color or effect. Deselect the group.

5. In the **Tools** panel, click on the arrow of the new **Shape Builder Tool** and select the **Live Paint Selection Tool.** ⬛5

6. Pass the mouse cursor over different areas of the rectangular grid with this active tool, and convert the Live Paint group. Apart from changing the shape if you place it on a face or an edge, each of these areas are colored in red. ⬛6 Click on one face of the grid to select it ⬛7 (you can increase the display zoom to work more comfortably).

7. You can select different faces at once. To do this, press the **Shift** key and, without releasing it, click on other faces. ⬛8

8. In the same way, you can select the edges that you need to modify. With the help of the **Live Paint Selection Tool**, click on some of the edges, which separate the faces of the grid, while holding down the **Shift** key. ⬛9

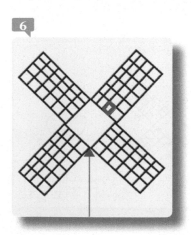

Coloring Live Paint groups

THE LIVE PAINT BUCKET TOOL colors the faces and edges of Live Paint groups with the selected paint attributes.

1. In the previous exercise you learned how to create a Live Paint group. In this exercise, you will learn how to paint faces and edges of a Live Paint group. You need to select a fill color. To do this, in the **Tools** panel, double-click on the swatch of this attribute.

2. In the **Color Picker** dialog box, select a blue tone from the vertical swatch bar, select the color you want in the left box and press **OK** to confirm the change.

3. From the **Options Bar**, choose a new path color. Display the **Stroke** field and in the **Swatches** panel, click on the swatch you want. New to the CS6 version of Illustrator is the ability to press the **Shift** key and access the alternate color picker that allows you to select a color by its hexadecimal values.

4. Since you already have the new fill and stroke colors, you can start to paint the object. In the **Tools** panel, click on the arrow

The selection of the fill color can also be carried out in the **Fill** field in the Options Bar.

of the **Live Paint Selection Tool** and select the **Live Paint Bucket Tool.**

5. In order to fill one of the faces of the group, click on it.

6. Repeat the action on other random faces of the grid and check the result.

7. Suppose you want to paint faces or parts of the object that belong together. Click on one of the faces and, without releasing the mouse button, drag the pointer over the rest that you want to paint.

8. The **Live Paint Bucket Tool** can also be configured to paint the fill and the edge or stroke of the group at the same time. Double-click on that tool.

9. This opens the **Live Paint Bucket Options** dialog box. In this box, click on the check mark for the **Paint Strokes** option and press **OK.**

10. As you place the cursor on any edge of the grid, the pointer changes, in this case into a brush. Click to apply the selected color. Repeat this action to paint the three remaining edges of the face and finish this exercise by changing the fill and stroke colors of the grid according to your preferences.

036

IMPORTANT

If you press the **Shift** key, you can change the paint mode of the Live Paint Bucket Tool (from fill to stroke or vice versa) without accessing the tool's Options box.

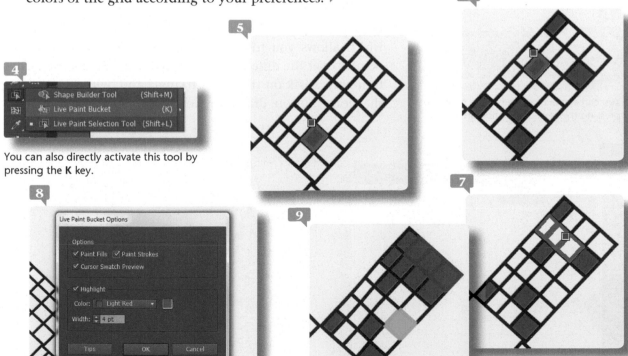

You can also directly activate this tool by pressing the **K** key.

The Shape Builder Tool

IMPORTANT

Double-click on the **Shape Builder Tool** to access its settings and customize the gap detection, coloring source, and highlighting according to your preferences.

WITH THE ILLUSTRATOR CS6'S SHAPE BUILDER TOOL it is possible to create complex shapes by merging and erasing simpler shapes. When activated, it intuitively highlights edges and regions of the selected object, which can be merged or eliminated to create new shapes.

1. In this exercise, you will learn how useful this Illustrator CS6 tool, the **Shape Builder**, with which you can easily merge simple shapes to obtain more complex ones, is. You will work with the **Project3.ai** file, which you can download from our website and copy into your documents folder. In this file are several overlapping triangles and a yellow star. Combine these shapes. Select the objects you want to merge. With the help of the **Selection Tool** and while holding down the **Shift** key, click on the first three triangles from the bottom.

2. Click on the arrow of the **Live Paint Bucket tool** and select the **Shape Builder Tool.**

3. By default, the tool is activated in the combination mode, which allows you to merge different paths. By placing the pointer over the different shapes that can be combined, they turn gray. Click on the lower triangle and, without releasing the mouse button, drag it up until the three selected triangles

You can also activate the Shape Builder by pressing the key combination **Shift + M**.

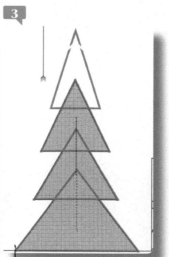

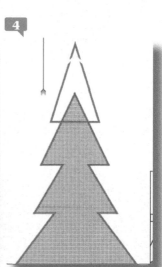

are highlighted in red. [3] As you release the mouse button, these shapes will become one. [4]

4. You will combine the new shape with the remaining triangle. Hold down the **Shift** key, with the **Selection Tool**, click on the triangle.

5. Activate the **Shape Builder tool** again and move the mouse pointer over the selected objects in order to see what shapes can be combined.

6. As already mentioned, the **Shape Builder** is enabled by default in Combination mode, but you can quickly move to the **Erase** mode by pressing the **Alt** key. Hold down that key and, after observing the change of the shape of the pointer, click on the bottom element (the result of the previous combination) [5] and have a look at the effect. [6]

7. Undo the operation by pressing the key combination **Ctrl + Z** and combine the selected shapes. [7]

8. All you need to do is combine the tree with the star. Select the two objects with the **Selection Tool** again and select the **Shape Builder Tool.**

9. Now you can use the **Erase** mode to eliminate the tip of the tree from the inside of the star. Hold down the **Alt** key and click on the edge of the shape, which is inside of the star, [8] to remove it.

10. Deselect the shape [9] and save the changes.

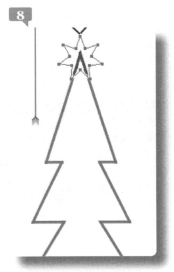

Note that the **graphic style** of the object being dragged, is applied to the combined shapes.

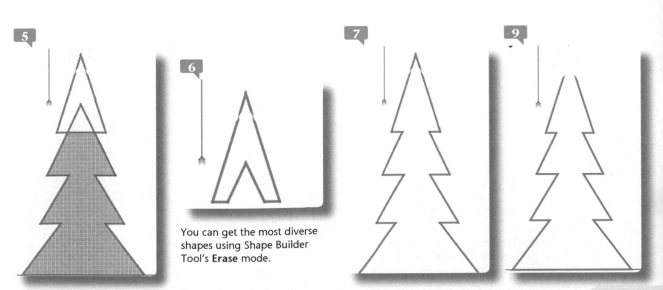

You can get the most diverse shapes using Shape Builder Tool's **Erase** mode.

Creating strokes with calligraphic brushes

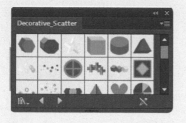
CALLIGRAPHIC BRUSHES CREATE strokes similar to those drawn with the angled point of a calligraphy pen, and they are drawn along the center of a path. The Paintbrush Tool applies to the last selected brush of the Brushes panel, where you can find all available brush libraries.

1. This exercise, which shows you how to use brushes in Illustrator, will work with the so-called calligraphy styles. With the help of closed paths, you will use this type of brush to draw a couple of holly leaves in our example illustration, **Project3.ai**. Click on the **Paintbrush** Tool in the **Tools** panel.

2. The method to create paths with the **Paintbrush tool**, is by dragging. Like that you can draw the shape of a holly leaf at the bottom of the illustration.

3. The **Paintbrush Tool** displays preset features that can be changed from the appropriate box options. To do this, double-click on the **Paintbrush Tool** in the **Tools** panel.

4. This opens the **Paintbrush Tool Options** dialog box. In this box, enable the **Fill new brush strokes** option to apply a fill color to the new closed brush strokes and press **OK**.

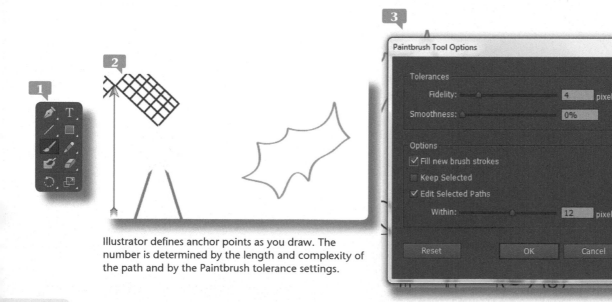

Illustrator defines anchor points as you draw. The number is determined by the length and complexity of the path and by the Paintbrush tolerance settings.

5. To see the effect of this option, select a fill color and create a new closed path. From the **Options Bar**, open the **Fill** field and select a green tone in the **Swatches** panel.

6. Draw a closed shape close to the previous one to obtain a holly leaf.

7. When you release the mouse button, the shape is colored with the chosen fill color. You will now learn how to access the **Brushes** panel, from where you can obtain all of Illustrator's brush libraries and choose from multiple shapes and sizes for these objects. In the group of collapsed panels on the right side of the screen, click on the fourth icon, which displays a tin with three brushes.

8. This opens the **Brushes** panel (which is grouped with the **Swatches** panel and **Symbols** panel). Besides being able to choose between different sizes and shapes of the default calligraphic brushes, you can also access an options box for brushes of this type from here. Simply click on the icon at the top right of this panel and choose the **Brush Options** command from the opening menu.

9. This opens the **Calligraphic Brush** options as the currently selected panel. Click on **Cancel** to exit this box without saving the changes.

IMPORTANT

Each calligraphic brush swatch included in the Brushes panel has its own O**ptions** box to customize each of these swatches in terms of angle of rotation, the roundness and the diameter of the brush.

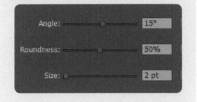

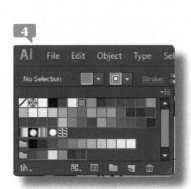

You know that you can also specify the fill and stroke color from the corresponding fields of the Tools panel and from the Swatches panel.

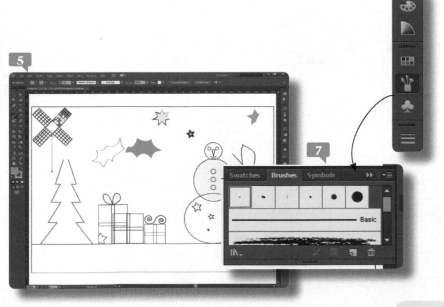

Using scatter, art, and pattern brushes

IMPORTANT

Remember that the Brush Tool, which is the last selected brush in the Brushes panel or in the brush library, can also be used as a Stroke Tool.

THE SCATTER BRUSHES DISPERSE COPIES OF AN OBJECT along a path, Art brushes change the shape of a brush or an object evenly throughout the path, and Pattern brushes paint a pattern, made of individual tiles, which repeats along a path.

1. In this exercise, you will learn about the effects that can be achieved by using scatter, art, and pattern brushes. You need to remove the chosen fill color from the previous exercise and create a new layer where you will place the new strokes. In the **Options Bar**, open the **Fill** field and select the swatch that contains a white background and a red diagonal line in the panel. **1**

2. Display the **Layers** panel by clicking on the next to last icon of the collapsed panels group, click on the **Create new layer** icon and rename the new layer as **Brushes**. **2**

3. Continue to use brushes by clicking on the **Brushes** icon in the same panel group. **3**

4. In this panel, click on the **Brush libraries menu** icon, the first one located at the bottom of this panel, click on the **Decorative** command and select the **Decorative_Scatter** option that appears in the submenu. **4**

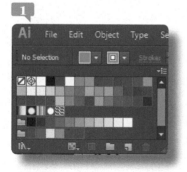

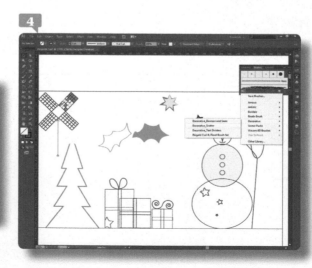

We recommend that once you get to know how these brushes work, to discover them on your own due to the immense and diverse choices that the program offers.

5. This opens the **Brush Libraries** panel, which displays the content of the selected library. Select one of the Scatter brush types and check if the swatch is added to the **Brushes** panel.

6. The use of these types of brushes is the same as the one previously shown for the calligraphic brushes. So click on the tree and, without releasing the mouse button, drag it down. (You can change the stroke weight in the **Options Bar**.)

7. The remaining brushes of the library belong to the art and pattern groups. Click on the **Brush library menu** command, then on the **Decorative** command and this time select the **Elegant Curl & Floral Brush Set** option.

8. The new panel appears on screen. With the help of this panel's **vertical scroll bar**, look at the wide range of art brushes in this group and select the one you prefer.

9. In the illustration, follow the path with the chosen brush by dragging the brush along the path.

10. An example of pattern brushes are ones included in the Borders Brushes group. Open the **Brush library menu** again, click on the **Borders** command and select, for example, the **Borders_Decorative** option.

11. Scroll through the long list of pattern brushes, choose the one you like and apply it to the artwork using the drag technique.

039

IMPORTANT

Remember that Pattern brushes paint a pattern, made of individual tiles, which is repeated along a path. These brushes can include up to five tiles for the sides, inner corner, outer corner, beginning, and end of the pattern.

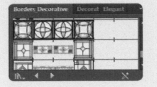

You can get straight lines using the Brush Tool by holding down the Shift key.

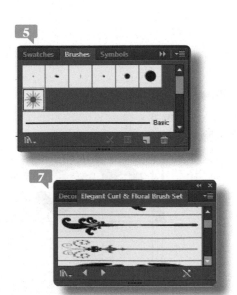

Working with the Blob Brush

THE BLOB BRUSH TOOL WAS NEW in Illustrator CS4 and allows you to draw paths with only a fill (no stroke) that can be combined with existing artwork with the same fill.

1. The combination of paths is extremely easy with the **Blob Brush**. In this exercise you will learn how to use it. Click on this tool in the **Tools** panel, which is displayed by the tip of a brush on some kind of stain.

2. Be aware that the Stain Brush acquires the currently selected features for the Calligraphic Brush. Choose red for the stroke color and, by dragging, draw several lines that simulate ribbon on one of the gifts.

3. With the help of this tool, the paths that make up the shape are linked and work as one, unlike what would have happened if you had drawn them with the **Brush Tool**. With the **Selection Tool**, click on the ribbons and watch how they are selected.

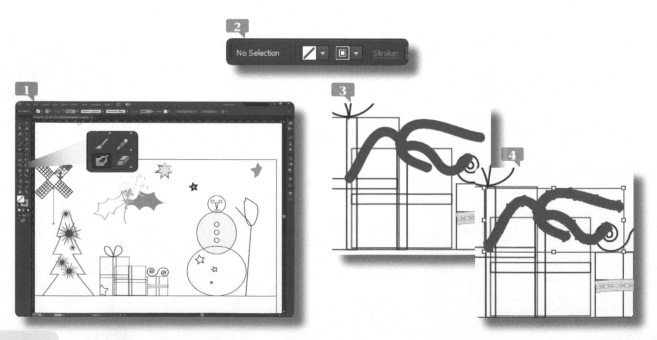

4. See in the **Options Bar** how the color, which we have chosen for the Stroke, now corresponds to the fill while the Stroke color is **None**. Remember that the **Blob Brush Tool** only allows you to create paths with fill, not with strokes. Change any of the features of the new path. Select the figure, open the **Fill** field in the **Options Bar** and select another color in the **Swatches** panel. **5**

5. Open the field that displays the **Basic** brush style and in the panel that appears, click on the style **Round** to **7** points. **6**

6. You have just applied a new path to your figure. Now you can see your changes in the picture. Click on an empty area in the artwork to delete the selection of the shape. **7**

7. Now you will learn how to access the Options box of the **Blob Brush Tool**. To do this, double-click on it in the **Tools** panel.

8. This opens the **Blob Brush Tool Options** box. The set options in the section **Default Brush Options** match the default settings for the Calligraphic brush. Click on **Cancel** to exit the box without making any changes. **8**

9. Save the changes by pressing the key combination **Ctrl + S**.

IMPORTANT

The **Keep Selected** option in the **Blob Brush Tool Options** box specifies that when you draw a merged path, all paths are selected and remain selected as you keep on drawing. This option is useful for viewing all paths included in the merged path.

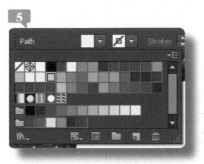

5

You can also select the attributes of the brush before drawing the path.

6

7

8

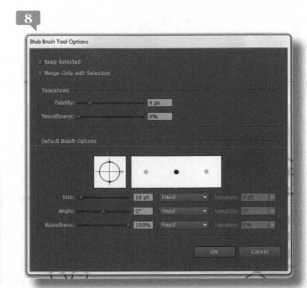

Drawing with the Bristle Brush

THE BRISTLE BRUSH WAS A NEW ADDITION to Illustrator CS5. With it you can paint with vectors that perfectly simulate real brush strokes, control the bristle characteristics (size, length, stiffness, shape, density, etc.), and the paint opacity to achieve very realistic effects.

1. In this exercise, you will get to know the Bristle Brush's functions, with which you create brush strokes that have the appearance of a natural brush. You will create a new customized Bristle Brush with which you will draw some strokes on illustration **Project3.ai**. Display the Brushes panel by clicking on the fourth icon of the collapsed panel on the right and select **New Brush**, the second command from the right at the bottom of the panel.

2. In the **New Brush** window, select the **Bristle Brush** option and press the **OK** button.

3. This opens the **Bristle Brush Options** box where, apart from selecting a name and choosing the shape of the brush, you can specify its properties. Call it **Tree Brush** and select the **Round Angle** brush shape.

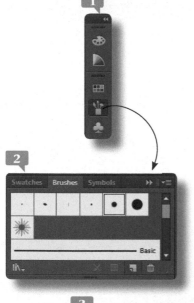

To access the **New Brush** box, you can also use this command in the Options menu in the Brushes panel.

You can choose from **ten different brush shapes,** and each of them provides a specific and unique drawing experience.

041

4. Set a size of 3 mm for the brush and a length of 50%. Choose a low Bristle density and a fine Thickness. (These are guidelines. We recommend you try them out and have a look in the preview at the different brush textures you can obtain.)

5. Choose a paint opacity of 35% and a stiffness of 25% and click on **OK** to create the customized Bristle Brush. 🔳5

6. The new brush appears in the Brushes panel. You just need to choose a color for the stroke and start painting. Double-click on the Stroke icon in the **Tools** panel 🔳6 to access the **Color Picker** box.

7. Choose a dark green tone and press the **OK** button. 🔳7

8. Paint the entire outline of the Christmas tree with this brush and have a look at the effect by releasing the mouse button. 🔳8

9. The **Bristle Brush Tool** is especially effective if you work with graphics tablets since a cursor annotator appears that simulates the tip of an actual brush. Further, while working with the mouse, only X- and Y-axis movements are recorded whereas features such as tilt, bearing, rotation, and pressure remain fixed, resulting in even strokes. We recommend you create new Bristle Brushes and apply them to your own images to discover their range. Finish this exercise by saving the changes in the illustration.

IMPORTANT

Illustrator CS6 provides a **library of preset Bristle Brushes** that can be accessed from the Bristle Brush Library menu in the Brushes panel.

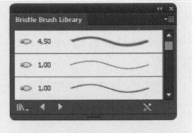

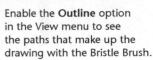

Enable the **Outline** option in the View menu to see the paths that make up the drawing with the Bristle Brush.

Applying gradients

GRADIENT FILLS APPLY A GRADUATED blend of colors. Illustrator lets you create a gradient fill and save it as a swatch to make it easier to apply the gradient to multiple objects.

1. In this exercise, you will learn how to apply gradients to objects and how to create a custom gradient. To do this, you will work on a new document called **Rocket.ai**, which can be downloaded from our website. Open it in the Illustrator workspace and use the **Selection Tool** to select the orange object that represents the fire from the rocket thrusters. 1

2. This will be the first object you will color with a gradient. At the bottom, the **Tools** panel displays the color mode applied to this object, in this case, an orange fill. To activate the **Gradient Fill**, click on the icon beneath the orange box in that part of the panel. 2

3. As you can see, Illustrator uses black and white as base colors to shape the gradient. 3 Once applied, you can modify the gradient to display other colors. However, in this case, you will learn how to create a new gradient and how to apply it later. Press the key combination **Ctrl + Z** to undo the application of the gradient.

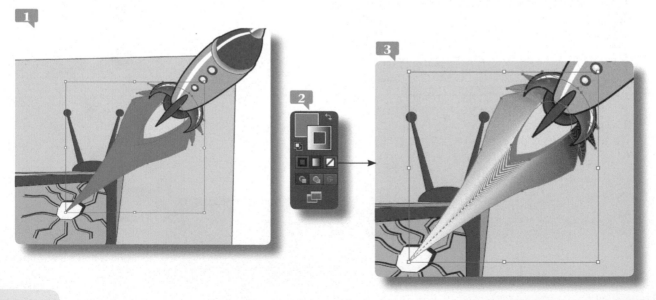

4. When you activate the Gradient fill mode, the **Gradient** panel appears, where you can create and edit gradients. In order to create new gradients, the first thing you need to do is to select its type: linear or radial. In this case, open the **Type** field of the panel and click on the **Linear** option.

5. See how the bar, which displays the gradient colors, is enabled displaying a small square at each end. From here you will change the colors. Double-click on the white swatch on the left in this color bar.

6. This opens a new color panel. Select a yellow tone for the origin of the gradient.

7. The update on the selected object allows us to instantly check the appearance of the gradient. Double-click on the end color swatch and this time select a red tone.

8. The small mark above the color bar allows you to locate the midpoints of the gradient, and establish more or less the quantity of each color. Select this swatch and enter the value of **35** in the **Location** field.

9. With the **Selection Tool**, click on an empty area in the artwork to have a look at the result and save the changes by pressing the key combination **Ctrl + S**.

042

IMPORTANT

In the Gradient panel, the icon to the left of the field (which allows you to change the direction of the gradient) helps you to invert the colors that make up the selected gradient.

You can also change the location percentage by dragging the color markers for the colors.

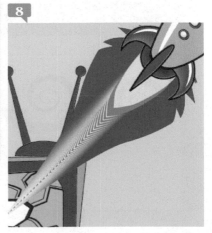

Use the icons on the left of the color palette to switch between the Swatch and Color panels.

Creating gradients on strokes

One of the new features in Illustrator CS6 is the new gradient on a stroke feature that offers a high level of creativity and variety whilst being incredibly easy to use. It offers total control over the opacity and placing of the strokes.

1. In previous versions of Illustrator, you could make gradients on strokes, but the process was long, difficult, and with too many steps that did nout always give you the desired result. In this new version of Illustrator CS6 the process is very easy to use and understand. Open a new file and create a form with the **Spiral Tool**, and edit it as you wish. When you have the form you want, Press the **Alt** key as you drag the shape to duplicate it twice, so you have three equal forms. You can also use the **Gradient.ai** located on our website. 🗨

2. Select the three elements and apply a different gradient to each of them using the **Gradient Tool**. 🗨 Apply the stroke gradient option. Remember that you can easily change colors and the points of color variation, as well as the number of color variation points by modifying the options in the **Gradient** menu. 🗨

3. Select one of the three elements and modify the stroke in the **Gradient** menu. You should change the current active option **Apply Gradient Within Stroke** (the icon on the left) for **Apply Gradient Along Stroke** (the icon in the center). Observe the difference. The same color is used, but in this case, the colors follow the form and direction of the stroke.

4. Proceed similarly with the spiral on the right. Select it and, from the **Gradient** panel, modify the stroke by using the icon on the right; **Apply Gradient Across Stroke**. See the result.

5. Observe the difference between the three types of gradient. Mastering the use of gradients can be useful on other occasions when applying this tool might be necessary.

6. What would happen if, instead of a linear gradient, you were to use a radial one? It is exactly the same; you will find three different types of gradient that are different to the linear ones. Experiment with it and observe the different possibilities that can be applied to the same form with one gradient color range.

7. To this variety of combinations, we should also add the changes in the thickness of the stroke, the form of the stroke, as well as the colors and the variety of different colors that form the gradient.

8. See the different effects with colors and gradients you can obtain. As you can see, the possibilities are infinite!

IMPORTANT

To modify the type of gradient stroke, the stroke type must be selected in the Gradient panel. To activate it, you must click on the stroke symbol (the empty square icon). If the **Fill** option is active, the apply a gradient to a stroke option is not active.

Creating radial and elliptical gradients

IMPORTANT

At the end of the list of gradient fills in the **Gradient** panel, you can find the Add to swatch icon, which can be used to save the current settings of your gradient as a swatch.

RADIAL GRADIENTS DISPLAY the blend of circular colors. When you change the aspect ratio for a radial gradient, it becomes an elliptical gradient.

1. In this new exercise dedicated to gradients, you will learn how you can create a radial gradient and convert it into an elliptical gradient. Use the **Rocket.ai** file, on which you will apply the new gradient. But first, increase the zoom display at the top of the rocket using the **Zoom Tool**.

2. Select the **Selection Tool** and click on the yellow ellipse drawn on this part of the rocket.

3. Use the **Gradient** panel to apply radial as well as linear gradients. Click on the **Gradient** command in the group of collapsed panels on the right of the screen.

4. The panel opens and displays the last configuration of the gradient. Click on the **Type** field and select **Radial** from the option list.

5. The new radial gradient is created with the applied colors and attributes based on the gradient. You will modify these values

You can create any type of gradient, and, after selecting the Gradient fill type in the Tools panel, draw the desired figure. This figure will be filled with the current gradient.

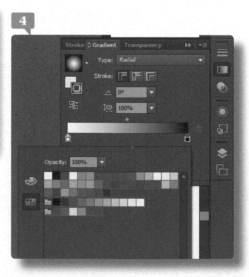

to create an entirely different gradient. In the **Gradient** panel, double-click on the swatch on the right.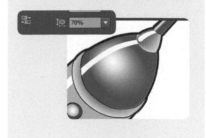

6. In the **Swatches** palette that appears, select a light blue swatch. 5

7. In this panel, drag the Gradient slider to the right so that the start color occupies the most space, and have a look at the result. 6

8. You will further adjust the aspect of the radial gradient. Double-click on the initial swatch and select, for example, yellow in the **Swatches** panel.

9. As a last change, you will reverse the colors of the gradient. To do this, click on the command below the visual field displaying the gradient type and observe how the gradient colors are reversed. 7

10. Click on a free area in the artwork to deselect it, and, after applying the new gradients to other elements of the drawing, save the changes using the **Save** option 8 in the **File** menu to finish the exercise.

IMPORTANT

To convert a radial gradient into an elliptical gradient, it is simply necessary to change the aspect ratio of it. The proportion is set to 70% in the **Gradient** panel.

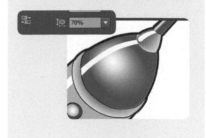

6
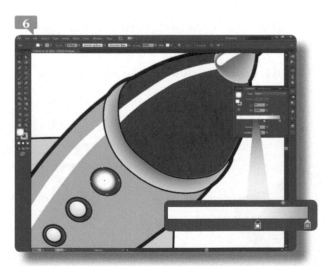

5
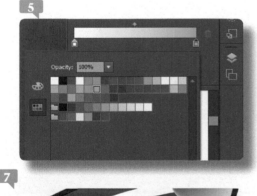

7
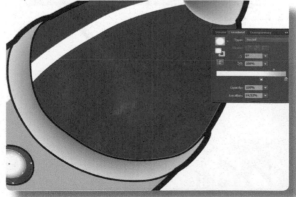

8

| Browse in Bridge... |
| Close |
| Save |
| Save As... |
| Save a Copy... |
| Save as Template... |

Changing the location of the colors, which are involved in the gradient, will obtain different and spectacular results.

Creating a mesh object

A MESH OBJECT IS A MULTICOLORED object on which colors can flow in different directions with a smooth transition between points. In fact, meshes are different from gradients in that the colors are multidirectional.

1. In this exercise, you will get to know what mesh objects are and how they are created. Create a new layer in the **Rocket.ai** file and rename it **Mesh**. 📮

2. Click on the **Fill** field in the **Options Bar** and choose a red tone from the Swatch panel. 📮 Create a new surface in the **Mesh** layer with the **Mesh Tool**.

3. Draw an irregular shape similar to the image on the green background of the picture, using any drawing tool you know how to use. 📮

4. In the **Tools** panel, click on the **Mesh Tool,** which is located to the left of the **Gradient Tool**. 📮

5. You will start to create the mesh object. To do this, click on the inside of the new shape and see what happens. 📮

6. The object converts to an irregular mesh object with the

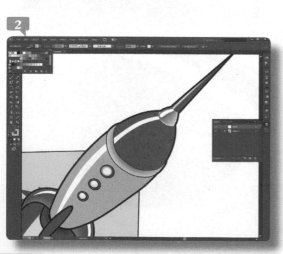

By clicking on an object with the **Mesh Tool**, you will convert it to an irregular mesh object, and its mesh points appear. If you cannot tell one mesh from the other, change the color of the layer.

minimum number of mesh lines. In order to include new mesh points, click on the object points wherever you want to place them. 6

7. After entering the necessary mesh points, the mesh object can be modified in various ways. For example, you can add new mesh points or eliminate the ones you consider unnecessary and change the fill color of the new points. To delete a mesh point, press the **Alt** key and, without releasing it, click on that point.

8. It is important to distinguish between mesh points and anchor points of a mesh object. Mesh points have the shape of a diamond, while anchor points have the shape of a square. It is also interesting to note that the object space, which is delimited by the mesh lines, is called a mesh patch. You can change the color of each mesh patch separately. We will show you one way to do it. Display the **Swatches** panel, which is the third command in the Panels collapsed group. 7

9. Click on the color swatch you want to apply and, without releasing the mouse button, drag it on the remnant you want to color. 8

10. In order to change the shape of some of the remnants of the object, simply click on one of the mesh points and drag it to obtain the shape you need. 9 Then deselect the object and save the changes.

IMPORTANT

In order to improve the performance and redraw speed, it is advisable to keep the size of the mesh objects to a minimum. Complex mesh objects can greatly reduce performance. Therefore, it is better to create a few simple and small mesh objects than to create a single, complex mesh object. When converting complex objects, use the **Create Mesh** command for the best results.

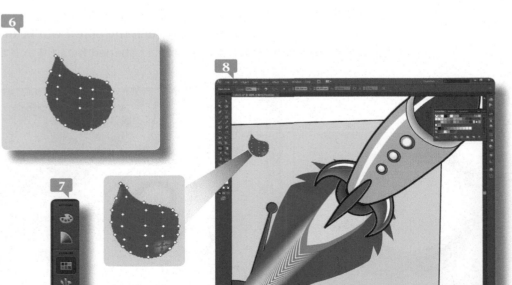

Change the colors and shape of the different mesh remnants of the object.

Changing gradients to mesh objects

ILLUSTRATOR ALLOWS YOU TO CARRY OUT a number of different conversions among mesh objects, objects with gradients, and paths. Remember that a mesh object is a multicolored object in which the colors can flow in diverse directions, with a soft transition between their points.

1. In this exercise, you will learn how to transform an object with a gradient into a mesh object and a mesh object into a path. You will begin by working on one of the rocket buttons to which you have applied a circular gradient. (You can download the file **Rocket2.ai** from our website if you do not have the up-to-date version of the document.) With the **Selection Tool**,  and after increasing the display zoom, click on the button of the rocket with the circular yellow and blue gradient.

2. Open the **Object** menu.

3. After having selected an object in the illustration, the **Object** menu displays an endless number of commands that will allow you to modify it in multiple ways. In this case, click on the **Expand** option.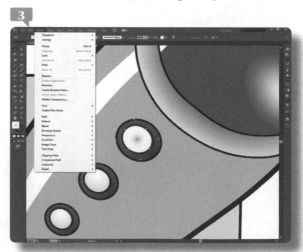

4. The **Expand** dialog box opens. In the first section of this box it is possible to select the parts in which the object will be divided. In this case, since it is an object shaped by a fill and a

stroke, you need to check both options. In the **Expand Gradient To** section, the **Gradient Mesh** option expands the gradients to one mesh object, while the **Specify** option allows you to divide those gradients into the number of objects that are specified. In this case, activate the **Gradient Mesh** option and press the **OK** button.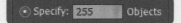

5. The selected object converts into a mesh object that takes the shape, in this case, of a circular gradient. To have a look at it, select the **Mesh Tool** in the **Tools** panel and click on the shape.

6. The **Options Bar** indicates that the circle has been transformed into a mesh or a mesh object. Now you can modify its color or shape by manipulating the mesh points. We do not want to finish without showing you how to transform a mesh object (the one you have created in the previous exercise) into a path. With the **Selection Tool**, click on the previously mentioned shape.

7. Open the **Object** menu, click on the **Path** command and choose the **Offset Path** option from the submenu.

8. In the **Offset Path** dialog box, you need to set the **Offset Path** to zero. To do this, type the value 0 in the **Offset Path** field and press the **OK** button.

9. The mesh points have been substituted by anchor points that only surround the object not its fill. Click on a free area in the illustration to eliminate the selection.

IMPORTANT

When transforming an object with gradient into a mesh object, it is possible to specify how many objects you would like to divide this object into by using the Expand dialog box. You should know that high values allow you to keep a soft color transition, while low values can create a color band effect.

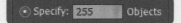

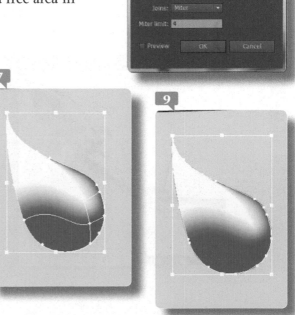

When transforming the gradient into a mesh object, it will display specific options.

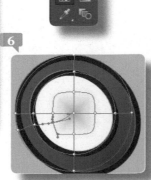

Filling with patterns

IMPORTANT

The patterns created to fill objects (fill patterns) are different in design and segmentation from the path patterns applied from the **Paintbrush** panel (paintbrush patterns). Further, fill patterns may only have one tile, whereas paintbrush patterns usually have five. It is recommended to use the first one to fill objects and the second one to contour them.

PATTERNS ARE REPEATED PATHS IN MOSAIC, compound paths, or text with solid fills or without any fill. Illustrator CS6 contains a wide palette of patterns in the Swatches palette and in the Swatch library panels.

1. Your goal in this exercise is to fill the green rectangular path in file **Rocket2.ai** with one of the patterns that Illustrator CS6 provides. To make sure that this object is located behind all the other ones, select it with the **Selection Tool**, open the **Object** menu, click on the **Arrange** command and select the **Send to Back** option in the submenu. 🔟

2. Now you have the rectangle where you wanted it. To apply a pattern fill, you should make sure that the **Fill** command is selected in the **Tools** panel and then go to the **Swatches** panel. Click on the third icon in the group of collapsed panels to the right of the window. 🔟

3. The **Swatches** panel displays by default all fill types that exist in Illustrator: color, gradients, patterns, and groups of colors. The last swatch in the fourth row is only an example

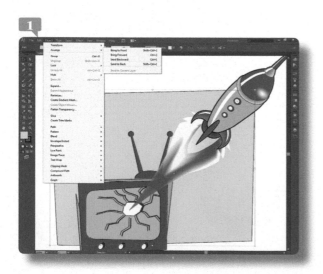

of pattern fills available. Display the Swatch library menu to have a look at the wide catalog of patterns it contains. Click on the first command at the bottom of the panel. ▼3

4. The libraries are organized alphabetically. As you can see, one of these groups, which is called **Patterns**, already exists although you should know that most of the other groups can also be considered as patterns. Click on the **Patterns** group, open the **Nature** category and click on the **Nature_Foliage** option. ▼4

5. A new panel that only contains swatches of the elected group now opens. If you locate the mouse pointer on each swatch, you will see the name of each one of them. As an example, click on the first swatch of the third row called **Petals Three Color**. ▼5

6. The selected pattern is shown in the Options Bar as well as in the **Fill** box in the **Tools** panel. ▼6 Press the key combination **Ctrl + Z** to undo the last action.

7. Apply another fill by clicking on its swatch in the panel **Nature_Foliage**, click on a free area of the illustration to eliminate the selection of the rectangle, have a look at the obtained effect ▼7 and save the changes by pressing the key combination **Ctrl + S**.

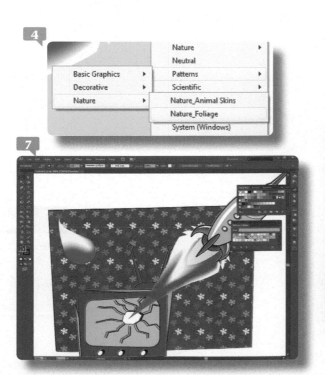

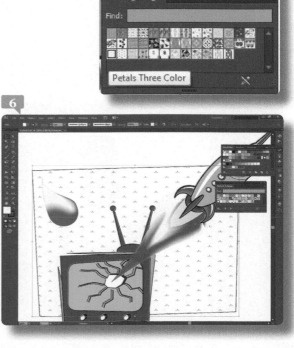

Creating your own pattern

ILLUSTRATOR CS6 INCLUDES A NEW ADDITION that allows you to easily create a vector pattern in the shape of a mosaic based on your own design. These patterns can be edited at any time and in such a simple way that it allows you to be very creative.

1. In this exercise, you will learn how to create vector patterns on a predetermined image. To do this, you will use one of the stars that can be found in the **Extrusion.ai** file. Open the file, choose the **Selection Tool** and select one of the stars.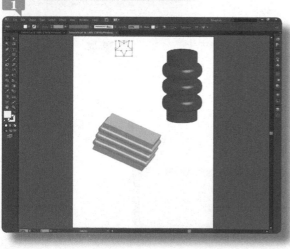

2. Select the star, open the **Object** menu, click on the **Pattern** option and select **Make**.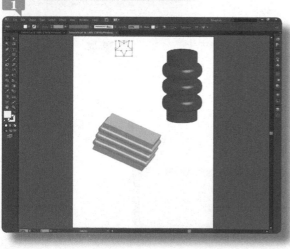

3. As you can see, your selected image is integrated into a pattern of repetitive images. It is now part of the **Swatches** panel, and any realized change will be applied to the swatch when closing it.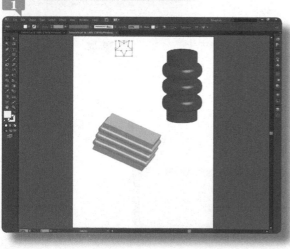

4. Select **Dim Copies to** and insert **50%** to see more clearly where the editable object is and to differentiate it from the copies that you have created.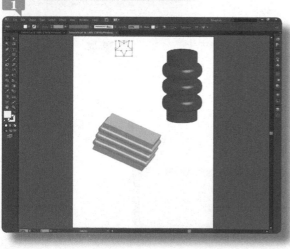

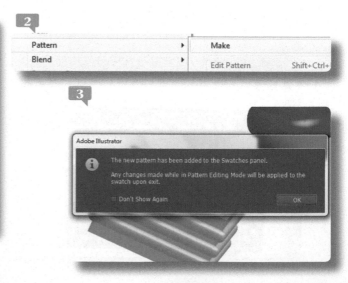

5. Group the images by using key combination **Ctrl + G** or by using the **Object** panel. Once the images have been grouped, duplicate the pattern and copy it lightly displacing the original so that a new design can be created. Use the **Color** panel and change the color of the second star to red. Observe how the newly created stars change.

6. In order to obtain an even more interesting design, vary the size of the second star. You can do this by using the **Scale** command in the **Object/Transform** menu or by dragging one of the figure handles. You can see that the changes, which have been made in the initial image, are realized immediately in the rest of the pattern.

7. A third star will be added in which the size and color can also be modified. Rename the pattern as **Stars**.

8. Once you are satisfied with the obtained result, you can change the **Dim Copies to** field to 100% as in the original pattern. To see the result, create a rectangle and select the new pattern as the background.

9. This will now be a pattern among the available ones in the **Swatches** panel.

10. Remember that this swatch can always be edited again and adapted as needed.

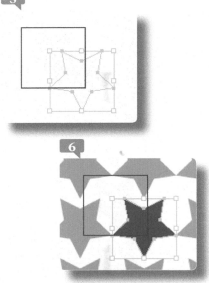

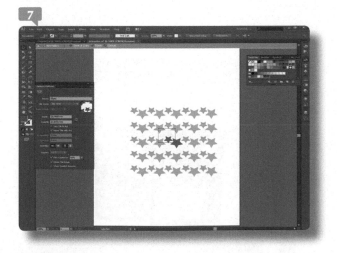

Reflecting objects

ILLUSTRATOR CONTAINS DIFFERENT tools to reflect objects: the Free Transformation Tool, the Reflect Tool and the Reflect command. When an object is reflected, a specular image is created across an invisible axis that is specified by the user.

1. In this exercise, you will learn how to reflect objects in Illustrator. To do this, you will use the different tools that Illustrator provides. First, you will group all the elements that make up the rocket and its flame. With the **Selection Tool**, trace a selection area that covers all the components of the rocket in the image. (Remember that you can add and remove elements if you click on them by keeping the **Caps** key pressed.)

2. Open the **Object** menu and click on the **Group** option.

3. Select the object, click on the central handle on the right-hand side and, without releasing the mouse button, drag it toward the left until the object is turned.

4. This way, you will obtain a reflection of the original object, although you will not keep this reflection in the image. Press the key combination **Ctrl + Z** to undo this transformation.

5. You will use another method to reflect the object. With the object still selected, click on the arrow tip of the **Rotate Tool** in the **Tools** panel and select the **Reflect Tool** from the list.

Transform
Arrange

Group
Ungroup
Lock
Unlock All
Hide
Show All

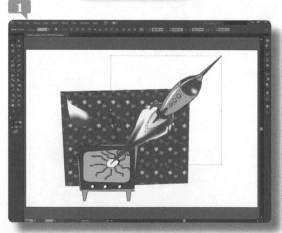

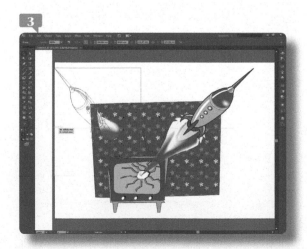

049

6. In this case, you first need to draw the invisible axis where you want to reflect the object. To do this, click to the left of the object.

7. In order to obtain a copy of the reflected object (which is what you need in this case) press the **Alt** key and, without releasing it, click approximately one centimeter below the first included point. **5**

8. You now have a reflection in your image. Keep in mind that if you had not pressed the **Alt** key when including the second axis you would not have obtained the copy of the object. There is also a third method to reflect objects. Press the key combination **Ctrl + Z** to undo the reflection.

9. With the object still selected, display the **Object** menu, click on the **Transform** command and select **Reflect** option from the submenu. **6**

10. The **Reflect** dialog box opens, where you should specify the axis from where you want to reflect the object (on a horizontal, vertical, or angled axis) and the type of elements that you want to transform. Keep all the options as they are and click on the **Copy** button to obtain a copy of the reflected object. **7**

11. Move the copy of the reflected object with the help of the dragging technique until you reach the point you want.

IMPORTANT

In the **Reflect** dialog box, you can select the element type that you want to reflect. By default, the **Transform Objects** element is selected. If you only want to reflect the patterns, activate the **Transform Patterns** option.

4

6

5

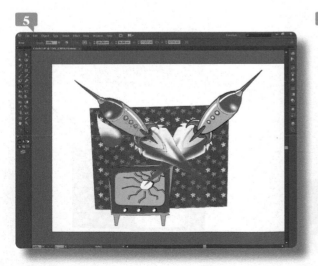

7

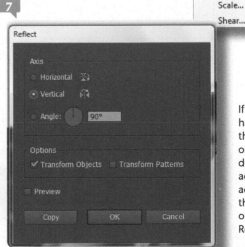

If you want to have a look at the reflected object before definitively accepting the action, activate the Preview option in the Reflect box.

Adding and editing text

THE TEXT FUNCTIONS ARE ONE of the most important aspects in Illustrator. You can add a single text line to the illustration, create columns and text lines, transform text into a shape or make it follow a path, and work with letter shapes as if they were graphic objects.

1. In this exercise, which is the first one especially dedicated to text in Illustrator, you will learn how to place text directly into your illustrations. It is important to know that the program also allows you to import text in Word and RTF formats. You will continue to work on the illustration **Rocket2.ai**. You will add small text in the upper part of the canvas. Select the **Type Tool**, which is displayed as the letter T in the **Tools** panel.

2. Click on the upper part of the illustration and write the following example sentence: **An explosion of images**.

3. Check if the **Options Bar** has been updated to display the fields and commands that are related to the text. Illustrator uses a number of predetermined parameters for the text, such as font and size. In the following exercise, you will see how to change this format. Click on a free area of the illustration with the **Selection Tool**.

An explosion of images

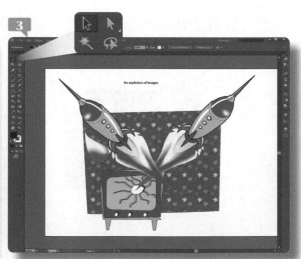

When selecting the **Type Tool**, the pointer transforms into an I-beam within a dotted box.

4. You will see that, once inserted, the text acts as a block. To do this, click on the text that has just been added.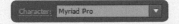

5. A line appears under the text and the **Options Bar** is updated. Click on the text again and, without releasing the mouse button, drag it upward.

6. As you have seen before, the **Type Tool** allows you to introduce horizontal text. However, Illustrator contains another tool that allows you to directly introduce vertical text. In the **Tools** panel, click on the arrow tip of the **Type Tool** and select the **Vertical Type Tool** from the list.

7. Click under the last letter of the sentence you have just written and write the following: **caught in time.**

8. Click on the **Selection Tool** in the **Tools** panel and click on the text that you have just written.

9. Press the **Shift** key and, without releasing it, click on the horizontal text to select both lines of text at the same time.

10. This way you can select several text blocks at the same time, as if they were objects. Adjust the text with the help of the direction keys in an area of the illustration that you want and click on a free area to remove the selection and finish the exercise.

IMPORTANT

With the Selected Type Tool, you will be able to configure the format parameters that you want before entering the text. This way, the text will be written according to these characteristics. To do this, you can use the Options Bar of the **Character** panel, which you can also access from this bar.

The small horizontal line near the bottom of the I-beam indicates the position of the baseline, on which the text rests.

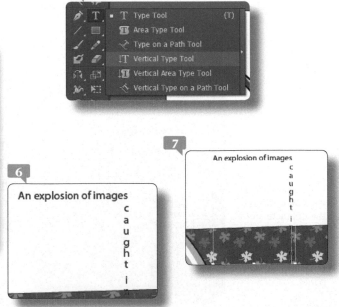

Formatting text

IMPORTANT

Keep in mind that when selecting a font color, the whole text that is being introduced will be written in this color. Check the text color in the Options Bar or in the Tools panel.

ONCE THE TEXT HAS BEEN INTRODUCED to the illustration, it can be modified in the letter type as well as its size, color, or alignment. The format changes can be carried out from the Options Bar or from the Character panel. In the new CS6 version you'll see a new menu called Text, which allows you to edit the characteristics of the text in a direct and simple way, in the Options Bar.

1. In this exercise, you will learn how easy it is to format text in Illustrator. Recover the illustration **Project3.ai** (remember that you can find this file in the download area of our website), type the text **Merry Christmas** in an empty area and select it with the **Selection Tool**. 🔲

2. Selecting the whole text as a block allows you to apply the same format to all the characters. Access the **Character** panel from the **Options Bar**. Click on the **Character** link of this bar and open the **Font** field, which displays by default the **Myriad Pro** letter type. 🔲

3. Locate, with the help of the vertical scroll bar of this list, the font called **Park Avenue** and click on it. (If this font does not appear in the list, it is because it has not been installed on your PC. Use a different font in this case). 🔲

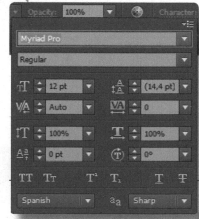

In Illustrator CS6, the edit options of the characters of a text are hidden in the Character link, which is displayed in the Characters panel.

4. The change is applied to the selected text at once. With the new CS6 version, a change in size can be realized directly in the **Type** menu by selecting the **Size** option. Use the **Character** panel again to modify the size of the text. To access this panel, this time open the **Window** menu, click on the **Type** option and select the **Character** panel.

5. This opens a floating panel that groups all functions related to the text formatting. Click on the arrow tip of the **Size** field and select, for example, **12 pt**.

6. In the **Units** category you can modify the units in which the size, the line spacing, and other characteristics of the text are shown. Open the **Edit** menu, click on the **Preferences** command and select the **Units** option.

7. The Preferences box opens showing the parameters that are relative to the units. In fact, you can see that the predetermined unit for the text is millimeters. These units can be modified to your needs.

8. The characters can also be modified independently. To check if it works, click on the **Type Tool** and select, with the help of the dragging technique, the initial letter of the sentence.

9. Display the **Fill** field in the **Options Bar**, select the color you like most from the Swatches panel and, with the Selection tool, click on a free area to have a look at the result.

You can also access the Character panel by pressing the key combination Ctrl + T.

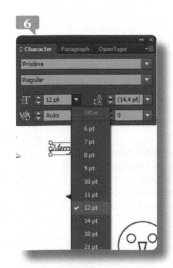

Working with long text

ILLUSTRATOR CS6 PROVIDES DIFFERENT methods to add long text to an illustration. The user can choose whether to write it into a defined area or to import the text from a file that has been created in another application. Illustrator accepts text that has been created in Word or RTF formats, which is characteristic of applications such as WordPad.

1. In this exercise, you will learn how to import text in Illustrator and how to add long text to a defined area. Before starting, we suggest downloading the file called **Text.docx** from our website and save it on your PC. Once you have it, open the **File** menu and click on the **Place** command. 🔲

2. The **Place** dialog box opens, where you should choose the file that contains this text. Locate it, select the **Text** file, and click on the **Place** button. 🔲

3. The **Microsoft Word Options** box appears in which you can indicate different specifications according to the text type that you will import. Since it is a very simple text, unselect the three options that are active in the **Include** section 🔲and click on the **OK** button to place the text.

In the **Microsoft Word Options** box you can also indicate if you want to delete the original formatting of the text.

052

4. The text is automatically placed into the illustration creating a text box or a delimiting area. The program locates the center of this box approximately in the center of the document. The next step will be to adjust this box to the space you want it to occupy. First, you will reduce the size of the box. To do this, display the **Transform** panel from the **Options Bar** and type **85 mm** in the **W** field.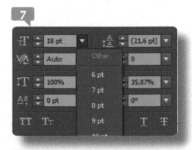

5. The box as well as the size of the letter decreases in size. You will change this size after placing the text where you want it. With the **Selection Tool**, drag the text box to a free area of the illustration.

6. Click on the **Type Tool** and select the long text.

7. In the **Character** panel, display the field font size and select a size with which you can read the text.

8. You will have a look at other configurable aspects of text in the following exercise, which is dedicated to the formatting application for paragraphs. Before finishing this exercise, you will learn another way of inserting long text in Illustrator. Select the **Type Tool**, click on a free area of the illustration and, without releasing the mouse button, drag it diagonally down to draw a rectangle.

This is also a delimiting area in which you can add the text manually with the Type Tool or place the text with the tool with which we have practiced in this exercise.

IMPORTANT

If you add more text than will fit in the text box, a small red square will appear in the lower right vertex of the delimiting area showing a + sign. This indicates that there is too much text. In these cases, you can choose to increase the size of the box, reduce the font size of the text, or create another box and link it to the previous one.

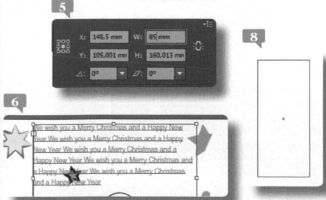

The **Type** menu also includes the necessary tools to modify the font and the size of a text.

Varying formatting paragraphs

AS WITH SHORT TEXT, long text added to Illustrator can also be formatted. Apart from changing the font, size, and color, long text can be aligned and changed according to certain parameters.

1. In this exercise, you will learn how to apply formatting to the long text added in the previous exercise and how to manipulate text that does not fit in the delimited area. Begin by activating the **Text Tool** in the **Tools** panel.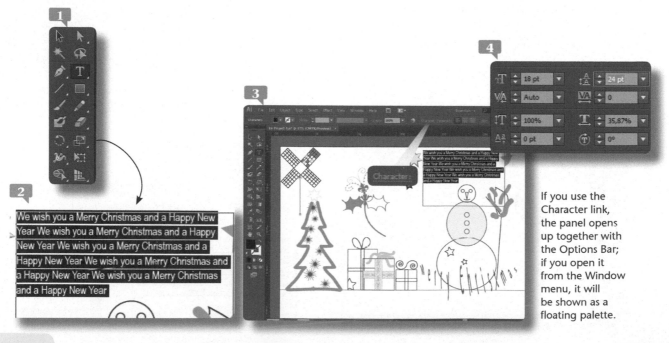

2. Click three times on the long text that was imported in the previous exercise to select it completely.

3. To change the spacing of the paragraph, you need to access the **Character** panel. Open it from the **Window** menu or by clicking on the **Character** link in the Options Bar.

4. The second numeric field in this panel is the one that defines the spacing (you can check it by placing the pointer of the mouse on the icon that precedes that field). You can enter an exact value in this field or use the arrow buttons to increase it point by point, and then keep on checking the change in the text.

We wish you a Merry Christmas and a Happy New Year We wish you a Merry Christmas and a Happy New Year We wish you a Merry Christmas and a Happy New Year We wish you a Merry Christmas and a Happy New Year We wish you a Merry Christmas and a Happy New Year

If you use the Character link, the panel opens up together with the Options Bar; if you open it from the Window menu, it will be shown as a floating palette.

053

5. The second aspect that you will modify in this paragraph is the alignment. By default, the paragraphs are aligned left without justifying. In this case, you will justify the text. To do this, you can access the **Paragraph** panel or use the alignment icons, which can be found in the **Options Bar.** Click on the **Paragraph** link in the **Options Bar.** [5]

6. The first three icons of the **Paragraph** panel allow you to align to the left, the center, and the right, while the four following icons are used to justify the text. Click on the first of these four icons, which corresponds to the justification with the last line aligned to the left. [6]

7. The lines of the paragraph occupy the whole width of the box. [7] The rest of the **Paragraph** panel fields let you apply indents to the text and spaces in front or behind them. See what happens when the text length overflows the previously defined box dimensions. Select the text and press the key combination **Ctrl + C** to copy it.

8. Click behind the last word of the text and press the key combination **Ctrl + V** to paste it as many times as necessary so that the text now does not fit in the box. [8]

9. In the lower right part of the frame a red box with a + sign appears, which indicates that there is an overflow of text. In this case, you have blank spaces that you can delete easily. Click behind the last word and press the **Delete** key until the red box disappears. [9]

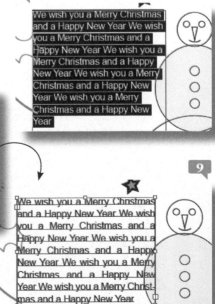

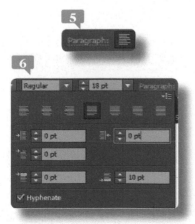

Remember that you can change the measure unit of the text characteristics from the Preferences box of the program.

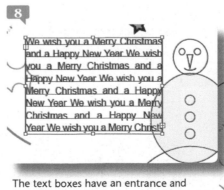

The text boxes have an entrance and an exit port that allow you to link them. When the exit port displays a + red sign in its interior, it means that there is an overflow of text.

Creating and using paragraph styles

A CHARACTER STYLE IS A collection of character formatting that is applied to a selected range of text, whereas a paragraph style includes character- and paragraph-formatting that can be applied to a selected paragraph or range of paragraphs. Using these style types saves time and ensures consistent formatting.

1. In this exercise, you will learn how to create a paragraph style and how to apply it to text. The use of styles is highly recommended especially in illustrations, which have a lot of text, such as in brochures or bulletins. The text in the **Project4.ai** file will be a good example to show you the procedure that you should follow to work with useful styles. You will begin by creating a paragraph style. Click, with the **Selection Tool,** on a free area in the illustration to delete any previous text selection. **1**

2. Open the **Window** menu, click on the **Type** command and select the **Paragraph Styles** option in the submenu that appears to open the corresponding panel. **2**

3. The **Paragraph Styles** panel opens to the right of the window that is grouped with the **Character Styles** panel. To create a new style, click on the **Create new style** icon, which is located in the lower right part of the panel. **3**

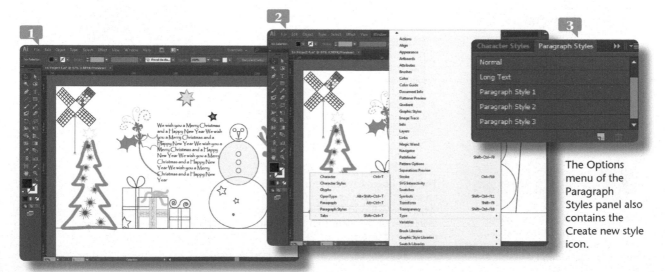

The Options menu of the Paragraph Styles panel also contains the Create new style icon.

4. The new style appears in the panel and is named **Paragraph Style 1** by default. Double-click on it to edit it. 4

5. The **Paragraph Style Options** dialog box opens, where you should specify the attributes for the new style. Remember that, once the style is created, you will be able to apply all the attributes by clicking once on the selected text. In the Categories list to the left of this box, click on **Basic Character Format**, select the **Park Avenue** font in the **Font family** field, 5 and choose a size of **10 pt** and a spacing of **10 pt**.

6. Select the left justified alignment in the category **Indents and Spacing**. 6

7. Go to the **Character Color** category and choose a green color for the text. 7

8. Write in the **Style Name** field the term **Long Text** 8 and click on **OK** to create the new style.

9. Check how the style is applied to the text. Select the long text in the illustration with the **Type Tool**.

10. In the **Paragraph Styles** panel, double-click on the **Long Text** style 9 and have a look at the immediate change on the selected text. 10

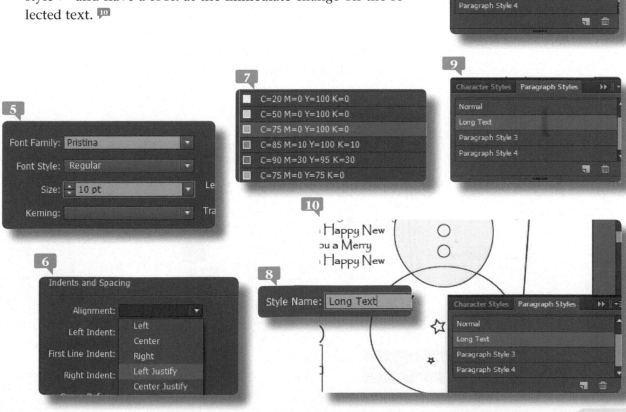

Varying the scale and rotating the text

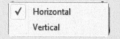
ILLUSTRATOR ALLOWS YOU TO TRANSFORM THE TEXT as if it was any other object. However, it is necessary to know that the way in which the text has been selected will affect the results of the transformation.

1. In this exercise, you will learn how to change the proportions of text and how to rotate it. You will practice with the **Merry Christmas** text that is inserted in the example document, **Project4.ai**. Select the text with the **Selection Tool** and drag it to the bottom of the snowman. 🔖

2. Enable the **Zoom Tool** and click a couple of times on the text you have just moved to increase its size. 🔖

3. Activate the **Type Tool** in the **Tools** panel and double-click on the word **Christmas** to select it. 🔖

4. You will modify the scale of this word, and to carry this out you will access the **Character** panel. Remember that it can be displayed as a floating panel from the **Window** menu or as a docked panel in the **Options Bar** by clicking on the **Character** link of that bar. Select one of these two methods. 🔖

5. In the second group of fields you can find the commands that will allow you to modify the scale of the characters. You should keep in mind that the scale change will distort the text, so it is necessary to be cautious with these transformations. Open the **Horizontal Scaling** field (which is displayed by the letter T with a horizontal double arrow under it) and select a value of **90%**.

6. The selected text is compressed horizontally. Subsequently, we will show you how to rotate a text. Double click the letter M of the sentence with which you are working.

7. Reopen the **Character** panel, click on the **Character Rotation** field, which displays a T surrounded by a curved arrow, select the value 30°. Have a look at the obtained effect.

8. You will now learn how to add an arc shape to this text. Select the complete text with the **Selection Tool**.

9. Open the **Effect** menu, click on the **Warp** option and select the **Arc Lower** effect.

10. The **Warp Options** box opens, where you should set up the options for this effect. Enable the **Preview** option to obtain a view of the changes before definitively applying them.

11. Increase the value of the **Bend** field to **75%** and click on **OK**.

12. Deselect the text and save the changes.

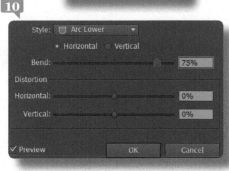

Converting type to outlines

ILLUSTRATOR TURNS ANY TEXT INTO A SET of compound paths, or outlines, which can be edited and manipulated like any other graphic object. Type as an outline is useful if you want to change the look of a large font on the screen.

1. In this exercise, you will learn how to convert type to an outline to edit it as if it was any other object. To do this, you will recover the document **Cover.ai**, with which you worked in the first exercises of this book. (Remember that you can find this file in the download area of our website). Open the **File** menu and click on the **Open** command.

2. In the **Open** dialog box, locate the mentioned picture and open it in Illustrator.

3. The illustration contains type, **My illustrations**, with which you will work in this exercise. To start the conversion of type to outline, select it as a type object not as a separate type. Use the **Selection Tool** to do this.

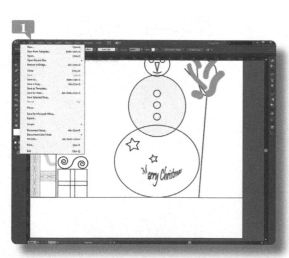

Remember that the **Open** command displays recent files in the **File** menu.

056

4. Open the **Type** menu and click on the **Create Outlines** command.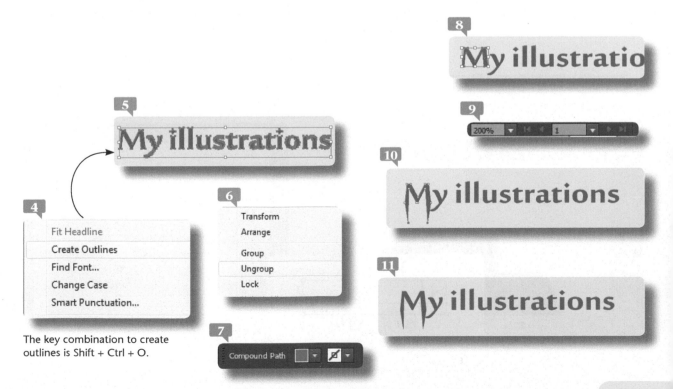

5. The type loses its original format. Nevertheless, all characters are grouped. In order to modify them separately as if they were an object, you need to ungroup them. Click on a free area of the illustration to deselect the outline.

6. Click on it and observe how the entire object is selected. Then ungroup it by opening the **Object** menu and click on the **Ungroup** command.

7. Check in the **Options Bar** if a compound path or an outline is in the foreground. Click on a free area of the illustration and click on the M.

8. You can now modify the letters one by one, as if they were separate objects. As an example, you will deform the selected letter. To do this, increase the page zoom by selecting the value 200% in the Display field at the bottom of the screen.

9. Use the **Direct Selection Tool**, click on the M again, then drag both ends down until the anchor points appear in white.

10. Click on a free area of the illustration to have a better look at the results and save the changes.

IMPORTANT

It is important to know that Illustrator cannot convert bitmap fonts to outlines or outline-protected fonts to outlines.

The key combination to create outlines is Shift + Ctrl + O.

Converting type to Live Paint groups

ILLUSTRATOR CS6 DOES NOT ALLOW DIRECT type conversion into a Live Paint group. To convert these items you need to convert type into a compound path or outline first.

1. In an earlier exercise, you have already learned about the significance of Live Paint groups and how to create these art objects. To summarize, we said that Live Paint groups allow you to treat each part of an object separately to apply different strokes and fills to those items. This exercise will show you how to convert a Live Paint group to a type object. But you have previously seen that this conversion is not possible on normal type, that is to say, one which has not been converted to a compound path. Open the document **Project4.ai** (or put it in the foreground if it is already open).

2. Enable the **Selection Tool** and click on the text **Merry Christmas** to which you have applied an arc effect.

3. Open the **Object** menu, click in the appearing submenu on the **Live Paint** command and check that the **Make** option is disabled.

126

057

4. This means that the selected object, in this case the type, cannot be converted directly to a Live Paint group. As already said, you can complete this conversion by converting the type first to a compound path or outline. Since you have already carried out this process in the previous exercise, you will use the mentioned object. Place it again in the illustration **Portada.ai** by clicking on its tab. 4

5. Enable the **Selection Tool**, trace a rectangle that delimits the entire **My illustrations** text and select it. 5

6. It is important to check the name of the selected object in the Options Bar (Compound Path). Now you can continue with the conversion of type to Live Paint groups. To do this, open the **Object** menu, click, in the appearing submenu, on the **Live Paint** command and click on the **Make** option. 6

7. Once again, have a look at the change in the **Options Bar,** which now displays the **Live Paint** name. 7 The conversion was carried out successfully. Now you can paint each letter separately, applying strokes and fills according to your preferences. Click on a free area of the illustration to remove the selection of the group.

8. In the **Options Bar**, select a new fill and stroke color to apply them to some letters of the text.

9. Complete the exercise by selecting the **Live Paint Bucket Tool** 8 to color a few letters of the text. 9

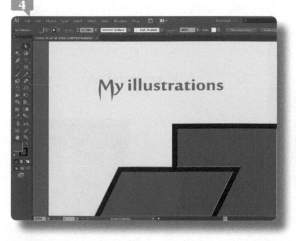

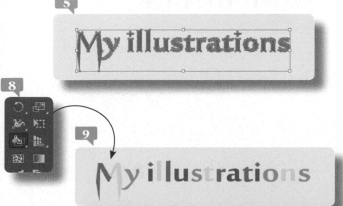

Applying effects to type

WHEN A TYPE HAS BEEN CONVERTED to a compound path or outline, you can apply multiple effects that provide originality and personality to the pictures. Among these effects is transparency.

1. In this exercise, you will learn about some effects that can be applied to text in Illustrator. To do this, you will expand the Live Paint group created in the previous exercise to work with some of the characters individually. Enable the **Selection Tool** and click on one of the letters of the **My illustrations** text to select the Live Paint group. 🗩

2. Click on the **Expand** button in the **Options Bar**. 🗩

3. The content of the **Options Bar** is immediately updated. Open the **Object** menu and click on the **Ungroup** command. 🗩

4. Click on a free area of the illustration to remove the type selection.

5. We will only select the three s letters of the text. To do this, click on one of them and, while holding down the **Shift** key, click on the other two. 🗩

6. The Illustrator effects are grouped in the **Effect** menu and in

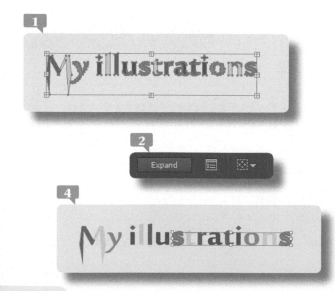

the **Appearance** panel. You will see how each one of them works. Display the **Effect** menu.

7. The effects are separated according to whether they belong to Illustrator or Photoshop. Since there are many effects available, we recommend that you discover the potential of these elements on your own. In this case, you will apply only a couple of them so you can see how they work. In the **Illustrator Effects** section, click on the **Stylize** effect group and select **Drop Shadow**. 5

8. All effects have their own Options Box, which allows you to adjust the different parameters for them. In this case, press the **OK** button to apply the drop shadow to the selected text with the default parameters. 6

9. Click on a free area of the illustration to have a look at the result. 7

10. With the help of the **Shift** key, select the letters **tion** of the word Illustration.

11. This time you will use the **Appearance** panel to apply a new effect to the type. Click on the Add New Effect icon, that displays a black circle in the collapsed panel group. 8

12. The **Appearance** panel controls all formatting aspects of the selected object. Click on the **Add New Effect** icon, which displays the letters fx at the bottom of the panel. 9

13. Click on the **Distort** effect group, select the **Diffuse Glow** effect and, after slightly reducing the amount of glow in the Properties box, click on **OK** to apply it. 10

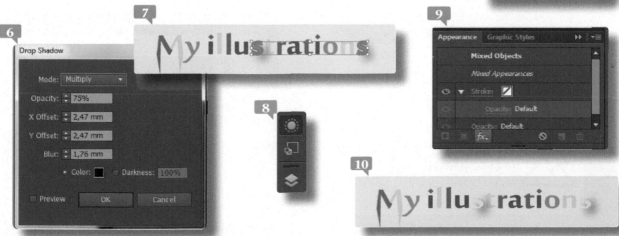

Wrapping text around an object

ILLUSTRATOR CONTAINS A VERY simple command to wrap text around any object, such as type objects, imported images, and other objects created in the application.

1. In this exercise, you will learn how to wrap text around an object. To do this, you will work again on the illustration **Project4.ai**. Click on the tab of this document to place it in the foreground or open it if it is not already open.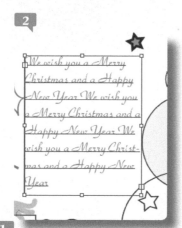

2. Your goal is to place the green type around the elliptical object that simulates the body of the snowman. However, the first thing to do is to place the text in the same layer as this object. Enable the **Selection Tool** and select the text box that contains the green type.

3. You will cut this text box to paste it in the layer that contains the snowman. Press the key combination **Ctrl + X** to cut the type box.

4. Display the **Layers** panel by clicking on the next to last icon of the docked elements panel, check if you are in the layer called **Brushes** and click on **Layer 1**, which contains the snowman.

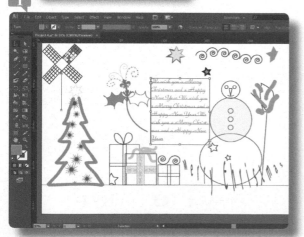

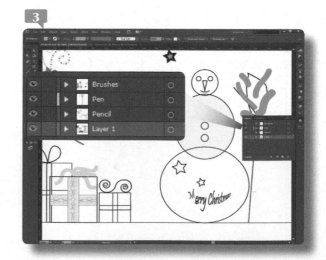

5. To copy the cut text fragment in the same place where it was but in the selected layer, open the **Edit** menu and select the **Paste in Place** option. 💬4

6. The last step before carrying out the process of wrapping the text around the object is to place the type object right below the object you want to wrap in the **Layers** panel. In the **Layers** panel, click on the arrow tip that precedes **Layer 1**.

7. In that panel, click on the type object you are manipulating (which begins with the words **Os deseamos**) and, without releasing the mouse button, drag it down to place it under the object called Path, which displays a blue fill color. (You have to scroll way down the drawn elements list in the layer.) 💬5

8. Drag the selected text until it is placed above the body of the snowman. 💬6

9. Select the figure with the **Selection Tool**, open the **Object** menu, click on the **Text Wrap** command and select the **Create** option.

10. The text wraps around the selected object. Once the text has wrapped, you can set several options for the effect. To do this, select the object, reopen the **Object** menu, click on the **Text Wrap** command and select **Text Wrap Options.**

11. In the Options Box, you can modify the displacement, that is, the amount of space between the text and the surrounding object, as well as the side of the object on which the type will be wrapped. Increase the displacement to **8mm**, 💬7 and click on **OK** to have a look at the result. 💬8

IMPORTANT

Once you have created a text area and removed its selection, and you cannot find it, select the layer you are working with, place the Selection Tool on the area until it is highlighted, and click on it to select it.

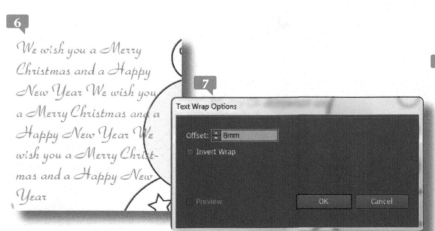

Entering text on a path

THE TYPE ON A PATH TOOL allows you to enter text along a path (which was previously created) with one of the tools available in Illustrator: a curved line, a wave, a spiral, a geometric figure, etc.

1. In the previous exercise, you saw how to wrap text around an object. In this exercise, you will learn how to create text that wraps around a path. Your goal is to enter text that is wrapped around a spiral-shaped path that you have previously created in a new layer. In the **Layers** panel, create a new layer and rename it **Type on a Path**.

2. Draw the spiral that will serve as the path for the effect. To do this, click on the arrow tip of the **Line Segment Tool** in the **Tools** panel, and select from the list the **Spiral Tool**.

3. Since it is not important to establish a specific shape for the spiral, you will draw directly on the figure. Nevertheless, remember that by clicking on the workspace, the Options dialog box for the tools is displayed. Click on a free area of the illustration and, without releasing the mouse button, drag diagonally to draw the spiral.

4. You already have the path that will serve as a guide for the text. Open the **Type Tool** in the **Tools** panel and select the **Type on a Path** option.

5. You can now start writing. To do this, click on one of the ends of the spiral and write repeatedly the phrase **Happy Holidays** until the path is filled.

6. Once entered, you can change the features of the text in multiple ways: from modifying its size and color to applying the most daring effects as you will see in the following exercise. In this case, you will change the color and apply a degree of transparency. To do this, select the **Type Tool** and triple-click on the text.

7. Open the **Fill** field in the **Options Bar** and choose the color your prefer from the Swatches panel.

8. Click on the **Opacity** link in the **Options Bar**.

9. The **Transparency** panel opens and displays a default value of 100% opacity. Use the slider of the **Opacity** field to reduce this parameter to approximately **80%**.

10. With the **Selection Tool**, click a free area of the illustration to have a better look at the result and finish by saving the changes.

060

IMPORTANT

Keep in mind that you can create text on open or closed paths and enter it vertically as well as horizontally.

133

Applying effects to text on a path

ALTHOUGH TEXT ON A PATH is very attractive and original, you can choose to apply different effects to the text. Nevertheless, you should be careful when you present text on a path with effects, since it can result in quite the opposite effect to the desired one and be overly decorative.

1. This exercise will show you how to apply special effects to text on a path. You will work on the spiral-shaped path from the previous exercise. Increase the zoom display of that area, select the **Type on a Path Tool**, and triple-click on the text to select it.

2. Open the **Type** menu and click on the **Type on a Path** command.

3. As you can see, there are five effects applicable: **Rainbow** (selected by default), **Skew**, **3D Ribbon**, **Stair Step**, and **Gravity**. As an example, click on the **Skew** effect.

4. With the **Selection Tool**, click a free area of the illustration to have a better look at the result.

5. Undo the action to apply other effects and observe its effect on the text. Press the key combination **Ctrl + Z**.

6. Reopen the **Type** menu, click on the **Type on a Path** command and this time select the **3D Ribbon** effect.

7. Keep in mind that depending on the shape of the path, the effect may not be appropriate and could prevent you from reading the text. Press the key combination **Ctrl + Z** to undo the action and select the text object.

8. You will apply the following effect in another way, although the beginning of the process is the same. Open the **Type** menu, click on the **Type on a Path** command and select this time the **Type on a Path Options** command.

9. This opens the **Type on a Path Options** dialog box, in which you can find the configuration parameters for the text (called Align to Path and Spacing) as well as the field called **Effect**. Open the latter field and select the **Stair Step** effect.

10. Click on the **Preview** check box to have a look at the results before applying the changes.

11. Thanks to the preview, you can see the effect of the changes before applying them permanently. Reopen the **Effect** field, this time choose the **Gravity** option and click on **OK** to apply the effect permanently.

12. Click on a free area of the illustration to have a better look at the result and finish the exercise.

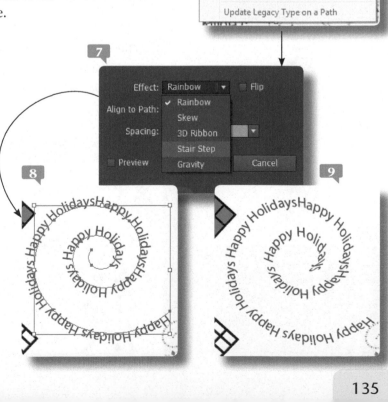

Organizing different layers

LAYERS LET YOU MANAGE ALL ELEMENTS in an illustration. They are like clear folders that contain objects. The layers are controlled from the Layers panel.

1. Although you have used layers in some previous exercises, this time you will learn how to manage them in the **Layers** panel in order to take full advantage of these organizational elements. Open the mentioned panel by clicking on the next to last icon of the collapsed Panel group. ▮

2. You have moved some of the objects of the illustration **Project4.ai** to new layers, whereas others (especially the ones we drew first) share the same layer called **Layer 1**. But if you have followed the steps of these exercises, your illustration should now have five layers. ▮ How do you know which layer occupies each element? Click on one of the elements, for example, the Christmas tree. ▮

3. The **Brushes** layer is highlighted in the **Layers** panel. In fact, this layer contains several elements distributed in sublayers. Click on the arrow tip that precedes this layer. ▮

4. The eye icon, which precedes each layer, allows you to hide and display the elements within the layers. Hiding objects is a way to work more freely, especially in these cases where ob-

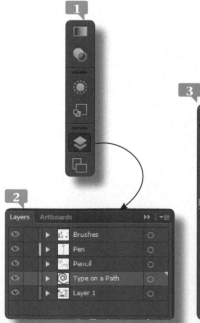

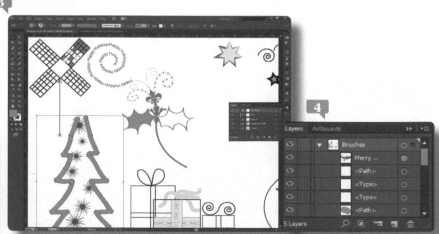

jects should be stacked up in the illustration. Here is an example. Click on the eye icon of the sublayer that contains the text **Merry Christmas**. **5**

5. The mentioned text is hidden, which does not mean it has been deleted. To display it again, click on the visibility box of this sublayer.

6. Illustrator sets no limits according to the number of layers it refers to; you can create as many as you need, and you can delete the ones you no longer use. You will learn how to create a new layer and place in it an existing item in the illustration. At the bottom of the **Layers** panel, click on the **Create new layer** icon. **6**

7. New layers are always added above the one selected. **7** Double-click on the new layer to access the **Layers Options** dialog box.

8. In this box you will assign a name to the layer. In the **Name** field, type in the word **Tree** and press the **OK** button. **8**

9. You will place the selected object (the tree), which is located in the **Brushes** layer, in the new layer. To do this, open the **Object** menu, click on the **Arrange** command and select from its submenu the **Send to Current Layer** option. **9**

10. The object is now part of the new layer. To finish, you will learn how to delete a selection from the **Layers** panel. Click on the drawing with the spiral brush above the snowman.

11. Layer 1 is selected in the **Layers** panel. Scroll through the contents of that layer until you find the selected item, click on the trash can icon on the panel **10** and observe how the path automatically disappears.

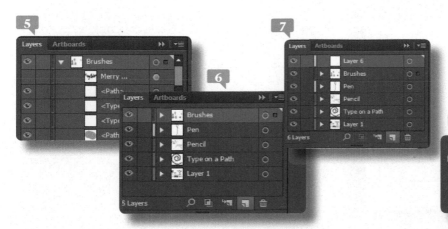

Applying revolving and extrusion to give depth

ILLUSTRATOR OFFERS TWO METHODS TO CREATE 3D objects from 2D artwork: by extrusion and revolving. Extruding extends a 2D object along its Z-axis to add depth.

1. This exercise will show you how to convert a 2D object to a 3D one. To do this, you will apply depth to the object by using an extrusion effect. You will work on the gift box on the right in the illustration **Project4.ai**. To begin, select, with the **Selection Tool**, the square and the rectangles that serve as the gift ribbon and group them by pressing the key combination **Ctrl + G**.

2. Open the **Effect** menu and click on the **3D** command.

3. Illustrator contains three methods to create objects in 3D: extrusion and bevel, revolving, and rotation. In this case, click on the **Extrude & Bevel** option.

4. The **3D Extrude & Bevel Options** dialog box opens, from where you can configure the effect. The **Position** field determines the shape of the object's rotation and the perspective from which it can be seen. Open this field and select the **Off-Axis Left** option.

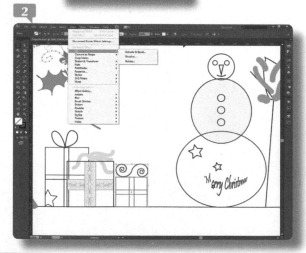

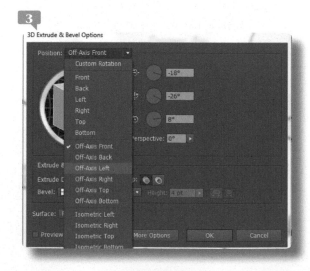

5. The example figure is displayed in the updated position. The three fields to the right determine, in this order, the degree of rotation of the X-axis (horizontal), Y-axis (vertical), and Z-axis (depth). Each position involves predetermined values. In the **Extrude Depth** field you can set the depth of the object. In this case, enter the value **60 pt**. 🔲

6. The **Cap** field specifies whether the object appears solid (first command enabled) or hollow (second command). Keep the option selected by default and change the appearance of the surface. Click on the arrow button of the **Surface** field.

7. Illustrator contains a wide variety of surfaces: from dull und unshaded matte surfaces to glossy and highlighted surfaces that look like plastic. Choose the **Wireframe** option. 🔲

8. Before applying the effect permanently, select the **Preview** option to have a look at the object's appearance. 🔲

9. If one of the assigned parameters does not satisfy you, you can change it now. Click on the **More Options** button 🔲 to display the lighting options that are, as we are told, not available for this surface type and press **OK** to close the Options box.

10. Deselect the object, have a look at the obtained effect, and then save the changes. 🔲

063

IMPORTANT

The option **Map Art** in the Options box assigns artwork onto surfaces of a 3D object. For example, you can assign a label or text to a bottle-shaped object or simply add different textures to each side of an object.

Map Art...

The depth of the object allows values between 0 and 2000 points.

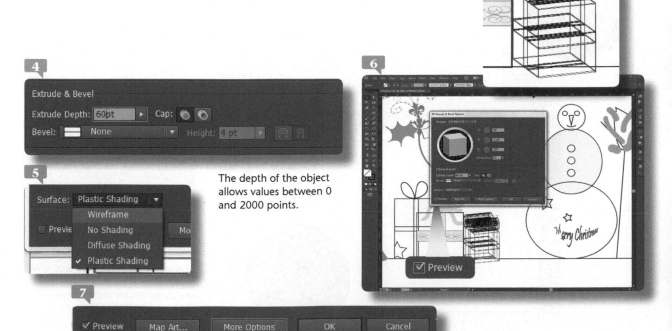

139

Adding bevels to extrusions

BEVELS ARE EDGES THAT ARE ADDED to an object where you have applied an extrusion. A bevel can be extended into or outside of the object, and the options can be specified in the Extrude & Bevel Options box.

1. In this exercise, you will learn how to apply a bevel to an extrusion effect. In a new white artwork, trace a circle with fill and without stroke by using the **Ellipse Tool** in combination with the **Shift** key. ▣

2. Apply to this object an extrusion effect with the default parameters by following the menu path **Effect/3D/Extrude & Bevel**. ▣

3. Access the Options box of an applied effect from the **Appearance** panel. Open the mentioned panel in the collapsed Panel group on the right side of the window. ▣

4. As seen in previous exercises, the **Appearance** panel displays all the effects applied to the selected object. Click on the **3D Extrude & Bevel** effect in that panel. ▣

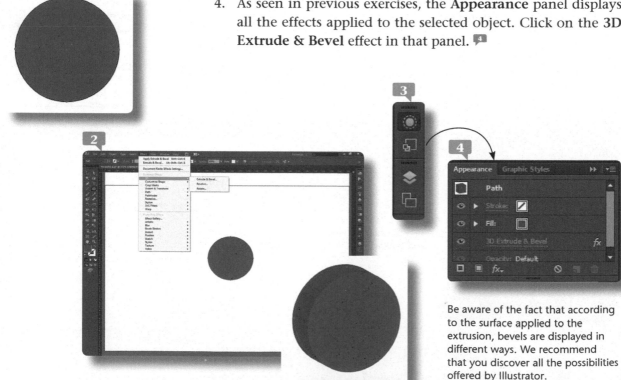

Be aware of the fact that according to the surface applied to the extrusion, bevels are displayed in different ways. We recommend that you discover all the possibilities offered by Illustrator.

064

5. You can find the options related to the bevel in the **Extrude & Bevel** section of the **3D Extrude & Bevel Options** box. Display the **Bevel** field, scroll through the list of bevel designs with the help of the vertical scroll bar and select the **Complex 3** option.

6. Click on the **Preview** check box to see the change on the object.

7. Increase the extrude depth to **300 points**.

8. The **Height** field sets the height of the bevel with a value between 1 and 100. Use the slider in this field to set a height of **20 points** and have a look at the effect.

9. The two icons to the right of the height field allow you to determine if the bevel should extend in or out. This option is selected by default. Enable the **Bevel Extend Out** option.

10. Before accepting the changes and creating a beveled extrusion on your object, change the object's position to obtain a different view of the figure in three dimensions. Open the **Position** field and this time select the **Off-Axis Top** option.

11. Press the **OK** button to apply the new effect, deselect the object and save the document.

If the height is too large for an object, it may cause the object to self-intersect and produce unexpected results.

Playing with the different parameters of the 3D Extrude & Bevel effect can convert a simple circle into spectacular shapes.

Mapping artwork onto a 3D object

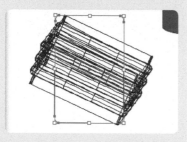

ALL 3D OBJECTS ARE MADE UP OF VARIOUS SURFACES. Illustrator contains an option that allows you to use other paths or illustrations as if they were material that surrounds the 3D object.

1. In this exercise, you will work with the green shape in the example illustration **Extrusion.ai**, which is, as always, listed in the download area of our website. You will convert the three stars that appear in this artwork to a symbol that you will use later to decorate the 3D object. Enable the **Selection Tool,** click on one of the stars, press the **Shift** key and, without releasing it, select the other two.

2. Open the **Object** menu and click on the **Group** command.

3. Check in the **Options Bar** that the group was successfully created. You need to convert it to a symbol. Symbols will be discussed later in this book. Display the **Symbols** panel by clicking on the clover icon.

4. Click on the objects group in the artwork and, without releasing the mouse button, drag it to the **Symbols** panel.

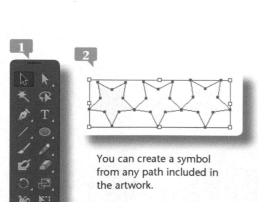

You can create a symbol from any path included in the artwork.

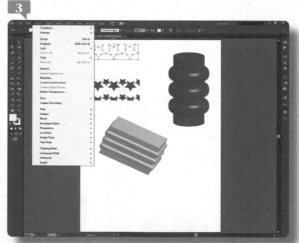

Apart from using the **Group** option of the **Object** menu, it is also possible to perform this action from the context menu of the selected objects or by pressing the key combination **Ctrl + G**.

065

5. In the **Symbols Options** dialog box, name the symbol **Stars** and press the **OK** button.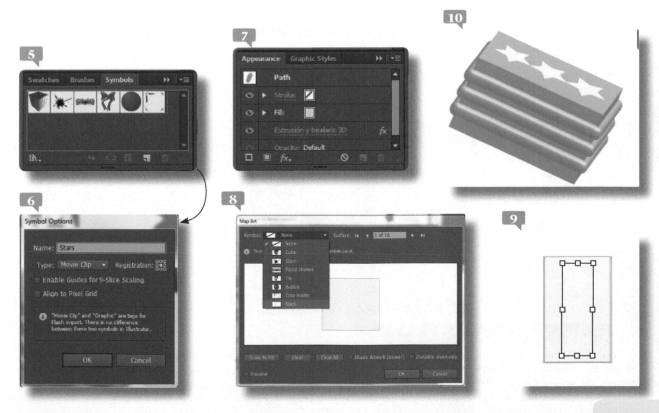

6. You can now start with the mapping artwork process. Select the 3D object, display the **Appearance** panel, then click on the **3D Extrude & Bevel** effect.

7. The **3D Extrude & Bevel Options** box opens. In it, click on the **Map Art** button.

8. The **Map Art** box appears, in which you select the object surface where you want to map the artwork and the symbol that you want to map to the object. Keep the **Surface1** layer of the object selected (in this view it is the upper face), open the **Symbol** field and locate and select the **Stars**.

9. To change the orientation of the symbol, place the cursor close to one corner and when it adopts the shape of a curved arrow, click on it and drag it to place it vertically.

10. In the two open boxes, click on **OK** and deselect the shape to have a look at the obtained effect.

Creating drawings in perspective

ILLUSTRATOR CS6 provides useful tools to facilitate and automate perspective drawing. The Perspective Grid Tool creates a grid in which you can draw shapes and scenes with a precise linear perspective of 1, 2, or 3 points. The Perspective Selection Tool lets you move, scale, duplicate, and transform objects dynamically.

1. In this exercise, you will practice with the following two tools: **Perspective Grid Tool** and **Perspective Selection Tool**. These two tools help to create scenes with realistic depth. You will start with a blank document with a landscape orientation. Activate the new perspective grid by clicking on the icon that displays that image in the **Tools** panel.

2. A grid of two points appears in the illustration with predetermined properties that can be adjusted according to your needs. Thus, with the help of the controllers at the bottom of the grid you can modify the vanishing points, grid planes, horizon height, grid cell size, and its extent. For example, to reduce the height of the perspective, drag the top controller down.

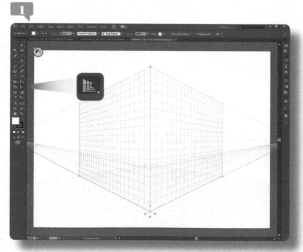

You can also enable the perspective grid from the **Perspective Grid** command of the View menu or by pressing the key combination **Shift + Ctrl + I**.

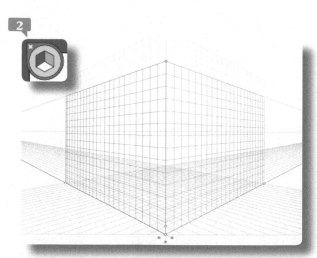

In the upper left corner of the artboard appears the icon that allows you to **change the plane**.

3. With the enabled perspective grid, any shape drawn with the drawing tools will be adjusted to it. Select the **Rectangle Tool** in the **Tools** panel and draw a rectangle in the left plane of the grid.

4. Apply a fill color and see how the shape adjusts to the grid. **3**

5. Activate the **Horizontal Grid** plane **4** by clicking on the icon that appears in the upper left corner of the artboard and trace a new rectangle with a different color from the lower right corner of the previous one. **5**

6. The **Perspective Grid Tool** also facilitates the creation of text in perspective. Select the **Type Tool** in the **Tools** panel and type the word **Supermarket** in an area free of the artwork, outside of the grid.

7. Select that word with the new **Perspective Selection** Tool and observe that when you place it on the grid, the characters are automatically adjusted. Click on the arrow tip of the **Perspective Grid Tool** and select the **Perspective Selection Tool**. **6**

8. Enable the left grid, drag the text and place it on the rectangle with the larger size you drew before.

9. Change the size and position of the text (keep the Perspective Selection Tool enabled) and see how they adjust themselves, taking into account the perspective. **7**

IMPORTANT

By default, Illustrator CS6 provides three perspective grid preset settings. You can save the new personal settings that are displayed in the Define Perspective Grid Presets box, and which are accessible from the **Edit** menu.

Presets:

[1P-Normal View]
[2P-Normal View]
[3P-Normal View]

4

Click on the **X button** of this icon to hide the perspective grid.

3

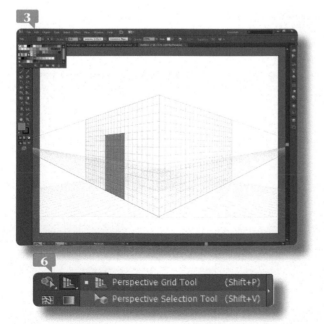

6

Perspective Grid Tool (Shift+P)
Perspective Selection Tool (Shift+V)

7

5

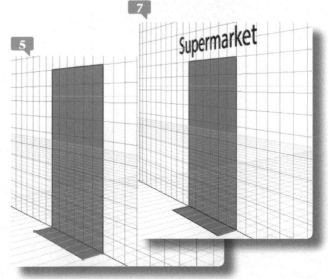

Blending objects

IN ORDER TO BLEND OBJECTS YOU NEED TO create and distribute shapes evenly between two objects. Illustrator also allows you to blend two open paths to create a smooth transition between objects, or you can combine blends of colors and objects to create color transitions in the shape of a particular object.

1. In this exercise, we will work on the illustration **Cover.ai**. Open it in the Illustrator workspace.

2. You will start by drawing a star, which you will duplicate by changing its color slightly. Open the **Rectangle Tool** in the **Tools** panel and select the **Star Tool**.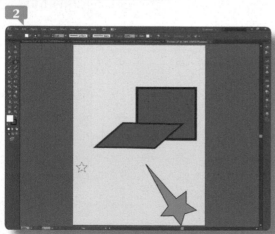

3. The star is drawn with the latest parameters for the tool. Trace the star using the drag technique.

4. From the **Options Bar**, apply a bright fill color, and increase the stroke weight.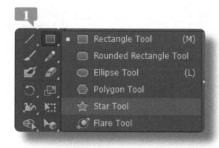

5. In order to obtain a copy of the object, press the key combination **Ctrl + C** and then press **Ctrl + V**.

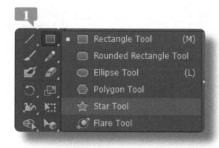

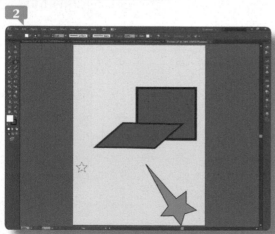

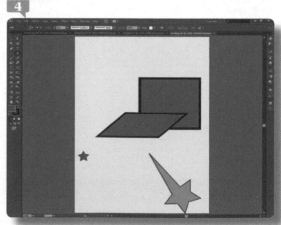

When you use the key combination **Ctrl + V** to paste a copied object, it sticks to the center of the artwork.

6. Enable the **Selection Tool**, click on the new star and drag it to place it about two inches higher in the same vertical plane. **5**

7. You already have the two objects between which the blending will be carried out. You can perform this action from the **Tools** panel or from the **Object** menu. The effect will always be the same. Click on the **Blend Tool** in the **Tools** panel. **6**

8. Click on each of the stars consecutively and see the result. **7**

9. Imagine that apart from this multiplication of objects, you want to obtain a smooth color transition. In this case, you need to specify this effect in the Blending Options box. Press the key combination **Ctrl + Z** to undo the effect.

10. From the **Options Bar**, apply a lighter color to the star in a higher plane **8** and double-click on the **Blend Tool** to access the Options dialog box.

11. In the **Spacing** box, select **Specified Steps** and enter the value 4 in the field to the right. **9**

12. You just need to repeat the previous steps. Select the **Blend Tool**, click on each of the stars and have a look at the result. **10**

IMPORTANT

You can blend objects of **different shapes and colors** to obtain spectacular effects.

You can also use the menu path **Object/Blend/Make** to create object blends.

The Blending Options dialog box not only specifies the number of steps that the program needs to create between both objects but also allows the distance between these steps and the orientation of the effect on the page to be set.

By default, Illustrator calculates the optimum number of steps to create a smooth color transition.

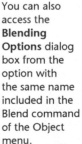

You can also access the **Blending Options** dialog box from the option with the same name included in the Blend command of the Object menu.

Modifying blended objects

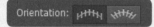
ONCE YOU HAVE CREATED BLENDEDED OBJECTS, Illustrator lets you edit the effect for different purposes: to change the path, change the distance between objects or stacking order, etc.

1. In this exercise, you will work on the blended objects that you created in the previous exercise to show you how to edit and modify them. To make the changes, you first need to select the object. Enable the **Selection Tool** and click on one of the stars.

2. In the **Options Bar**, see how the name **Blend** is displayed for the selection. The first change you will perform is to expand the distance between the steps of the blend. To do this, open the **Object** menu, click on the **Blend** command and select **Blend Options** from the list.

3. This opens the Options box. Display the **Spacing** field, select the **Specified Distance** option, and enter a value of **10 mm** in the field to the right.

4. More objects will appear like that and they will slightly overlap each other. Press **OK** to check it.

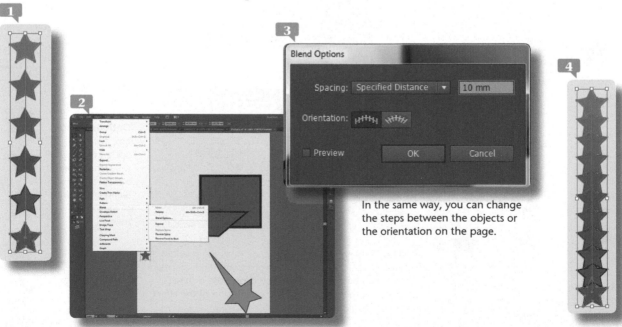

In the same way, you can change the steps between the objects or the orientation on the page.

5. You will perform another change on the blended objects by modifying the spine where the blend is performed. The spine is the path along which the steps of a blended object are aligned. By default, the path forms a straight line. You can change the current shape or create a new path and replace it with the existing one. Click on the **Direct Selection Tool** in the **Tools** panel 5 and click on the path.

6. Drag the anchor points of the path to change the incline. 6

7. Draw a new path with the **Pencil Tool** and assign the blended object to the spine. To do this, click on the mentioned tool in the **Tools** panel. 7

8. Draw a double curve or any other figure you like. 8

9. You need to select the two paths at once. Enable the **Selection Tool**, select the new path, and press the **Shift** key while clicking on the blended object. 9

10. Open the **Object** menu, click on the **Blend** command and this time select the **Replace Spine** option. 10

11. The replacement of the path is performed correctly. 11 You can also reverse the stacking order. To do this, select the object, open the **Object** menu, click on the **Blend** command and select **Reverse Front to Back**. 12

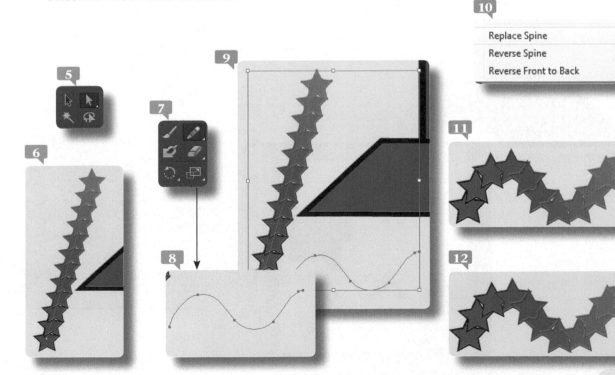

149

Distorting objects using an envelope

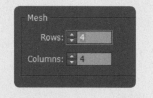
ENVELOPES ARE OBJECTS THAT distort or reshape selected objects. Envelopes can be generated from existing objects on an artboard or they can use preset warp shapes or meshes.

1. In this exercise, you will learn how to create objects with distorting effects with the help of these so-called envelopes. You will apply an envelope effect to the inclined rectangle located in the central part of the artwork **Cover.ai**. Select the object.

2. Open the **Object** menu, click on the **Envelope Distort** command and select the **Make with Warp** option in the submenu that appears.

3. This opens the **Warp Options** dialog box, which reminds you of the Options box from which you distorted text in previous exercises. Select a deformation style. Display the **Style** field and select in this case the **Flag** option.

4. After choosing the warp style, you can change the different aspects of this warp. For example, you can indicate that the warp should be horizontal or vertical, and you can define the percentage of curvature. Select the **Preview** option to have a look at the effects of the changes to the object.

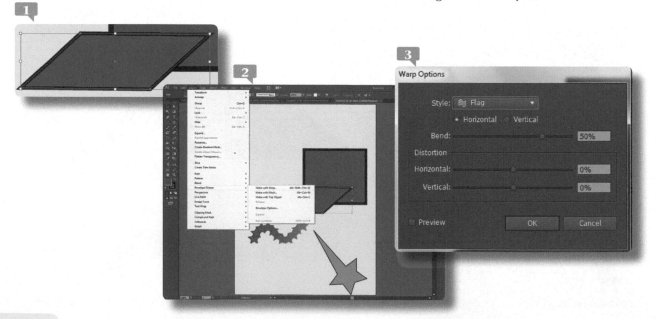

5. Click on the **Vertical** option button. 5

6. You can modify the styles as well as the orientation or the different percentages of distortion. As an example, reduce the curvature to approximately 29%. 6

7. Since we want to show you further possibilities with envelopes, apply the warp without any further changes by clicking on **OK**. 7

8. Create two new objects into two new layers, where one of them should act as an envelope. Create a new layer, draw a square with the **Rectangle Tool**, and apply one of the patterns available in the Swatches panel as a fill. 8

9. In a new layer, 9 draw a circle without any fill with the **Ellipse Tool** on the square. 10

10. You already have the objects that will be involved in the creation of the effect. To use an object as the envelope shape, make sure that the mentioned object (in this case the circle) is on top of the stacking order of the selected object. Select the two objects with the **Selection Tool** and with the help of the **Shift** key, open the **Object** menu, click on the **Envelope Distort** command and select in this case the **Make with Top Object** option.

11. Click on a free area of the artwork to have a look at the result 11 and then save the changes.

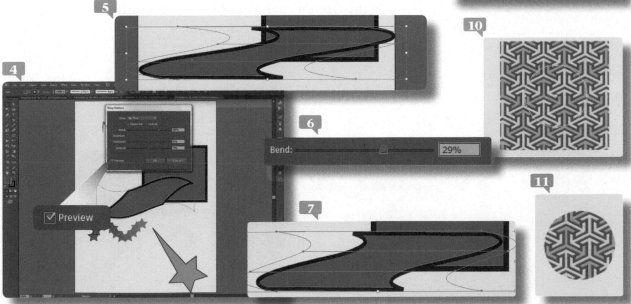

Editing and removing envelopes

IMPORTANT

If the envelope consists of grouped paths, you should click on the triangle to the left of the <**Envelope**> entry in the **Layers** panel to view and target the path you want to edit.

ONCE YOU APPLY AN ENVELOPE to an object, Illustrator allows you to edit, delete, or expand it at any time. You can edit an envelope shape as well as the enveloped object, but not both at the same time.

1. In this exercise, you will edit the enveloped shapes from the previous exercise. (You can find an updated version of the sample file with the name **Cover2.ai** in the download area of our website). To begin, change the content of the envelope created from a circle. First you will change the pattern. Enable the **Selection Tool** and click on the enveloped object.

2. The **Options Bar** displays all options related to this object. In that bar, click on the **Edit Contents** command that is displayed by a star.

3. The **Options Bar** is updated and now displays the characteristics of the envelope contents. In order to apply a new pattern, open the **Fill** field and select one of the available swatches, which should either be of a gradient or of a pattern.

4. Once the appropriate modifications have been performed, you need to return the object to its envelope state. To do this, in the **Options Bar**, click on the first button that corresponds to the **Edit Envelope** command.

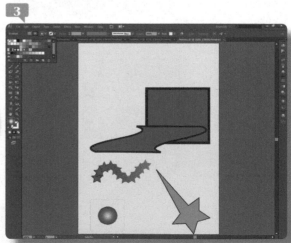

5. Click on a free area of the artwork to remove the selection from the envelope.

6. In the second part of this exercise, we will show you how to access the options of an envelope and how to remove it. Start by selecting the flag-shaped envelope.

7. When we talk about envelope options we do not refer to the attributes and styles applied to the object, but to the other options that determine the shape in which it distorts to fit the envelope. To access this Options box, open the **Object** menu, click on the **Envelope Distort** command and select **Envelope Options**. 5

8. The **Anti-Alias** option smooths rasters when distorted with an envelope. The **Preserve Shape Using** option specifies how rasters preserve their shape when distorted by nonrectangular envelopes. You can choose between clipping masks, which will be discussed in the following exercise, or an alpha channel of transparency. **Fidelity** specifies how precisely the object fits to the envelope mold. Press the **Cancel** button. 6

9. To finish this exercise, you will remove the envelope created on this object. To do this, you can choose to keep the object in the envelope shape or its original shape. Open the **Object** menu, click on the **Envelope Distort** command and select the **Release** option. 7

10. You now have two separate objects. Select the flag-shaped object 8 and press the **Delete** key to remove it.

IMPORTANT

Remove envelopes by either releasing or expanding them. Expanding an enveloped object removes the envelope, but the object retains its distorted shape. To do this, open the **Object** menu, click on the **Envelope Distort** command and select the **Expand** option.

Expand

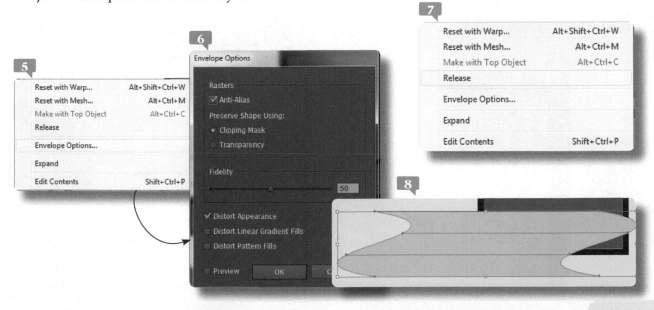

Using clipping masks

A CLIPPING MASK IS AN OBJECT whose shape masks other artwork so that only you can see areas that are within the shape, which is to say, clipping the artwork to the shape of the mask. The clipping mask and the objects that are masked are called a clipping set.

1. In this exercise you will learn how to create a new effect on the illustration **Project4.ai** using the so-called clipping masks. Clipping masks are very similar to the effects we discussed in the previous exercises. Your goal is to create a cloud from two objects. Create a new layer called **Background cloud**. 🗨

2. Select the **Rectangle Tool** in the **Tools** panel 🗨 and draw a rectangle at the top of the illustration. 🗨

3. Apply a light blue fill color to the rectangle. 🗨

4. You need to create a new layer and rename it **Cloud**.

5. Select the **Pencil Tool** 🗨 and draw a figure in the shape of a cloud and without any fill above the rectangle. 🗨

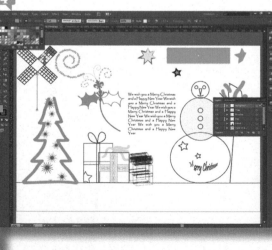

The object, which serves as a mask, is called a clipping path. Only vector objects can be clipping paths.

6. Now you have the two objects that intervene in the process. To create the clipping mask, you first need to select these items. Then to select the clipping path, choose the **Selection Tool**, press the **Shift** key and, without releasing it, click on the new rectangle.

7. Open the **Object** menu, click on the **Clipping Mask** command and select the **Make** option from the submenu. **7**

8. Notice what happens: a new object in the shape of a cloud has been created and with the background of the rectangle. **8** The clipping sets of the objects are combined as a single group in the **Layers** panel. In this panel, click on the white arrow tip that precedes the **Cloud** layer. **9**

9. After you have created a clipping mask, it can be easily edited from the **Layers** panel or the **Options Bar**. Select the **Cloud** layer, click on the first button in the **Options Bar,** which corresponds to the **Edit Clipping Mask** command. **10**

10. Now you can realize the desired changes to the mask. For example, open the **Stroke** field of the same bar and select the color black to assign an outline to the figure. **11**

11. In order to modify the contents, click on the second button in the **Options Bar**.

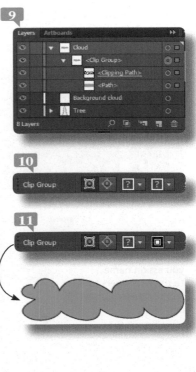

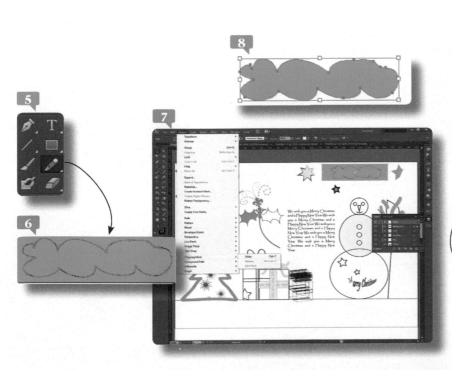

Varying and editing clipping masks

ONCE YOU HAVE CREATED A CLIPPING MASK, it can be edited and modified in many ways: Illustrator allows you to edit the mask and content separately as well as add or delete items of a clipping set.

1. In this exercise, you will continue to work with the so-called clipping masks. In this case, you will learn how to create a new mask from the Layers panel and then you will add new objects that you created in the previous exercise. Create a new layer in the **Layers** panel and rename it **Clipping set.**

2. You will follow the same steps as in the previous exercise, so you can obtain the same result following a different procedure. Select the **Rectangle Tool** and draw a rectangle in a free area of the illustration.

3. In the **Options Bar**, choose a fill color or a gradient and apply it to the rectangle.

4. Check if all new elements are placed into the selected layer. Choose the **Pencil Tool** and draw, with the help of the drag technique, a figure, which looks like a cloud, on the rectangle.

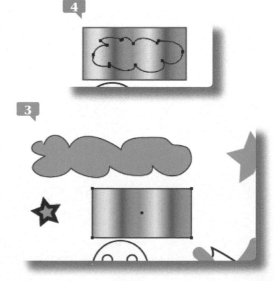

Note that it is highly recommended that you assign names to the new layers to identify them quickly and easily.

072

5. The cloud will act as a clipping path, so it is very important that this object is on the top of the objects group of the layer. Click on the arrow tip that precedes the **Clipping set** layer.

6. The last created object is automatically placed in first place, which means that you can continue to create the mask. To do this, and after making sure that the already mentioned layer is selected, click on the **Make/Release Clipping Mask** button, the second icon at the bottom of the **Layers** panel.

7. The mask is created as expected. With the **Selection Tool**, click on a free area of the window to see the result better.

8. Now you will learn how to undo a clipping set that separates the different elements. To do this, in the **Layers** panel, click on one of the layers containing the clipping mask to select it.

9. Now you can use the **Create/Release Clipping Mask** button in the Layers panel or go to the **Object** menu. In this case, open this menu, click on the **Clipping Mask** command and select **Release** from the submenu of options.

10. Now you need to separate the two objects that made up the clipping set. Remove both figures directly by pressing the **Delete** key on your keyboard.

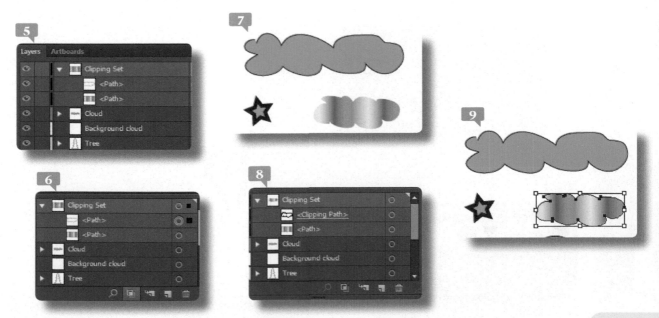

Adding symbols

A SYMBOL IS AN ART OBJECT THAT CAN BE USED repeatedly in an illustration. Each symbol instance (the object used in the illustration) is linked to the symbol in the Symbols panel or to a symbols library. Using symbols can save you time and greatly reduce file size.

1. In this exercise, you will become familiar with the symbols and the panel from which you manage these art objects. Create a new layer in the document **Project4.ai** and rename it **Symbol**.

2. Open the **Symbols** panel. In the group of collapsed panels on the right of the workspace, click on the icon that displays the image of a clover.

3. Illustrator contains six swatch symbols, which occupy the first row of the **Symbols** panel. How can you put one of these symbols in the picture? Just use the drag technique. As an example, click on the lasso symbol, hold down the mouse button, and drag it into position over one of the gifts.

4. The object within the picture changes from a symbol into a symbol instance, as you can see in the **Options Bar**. Dragging

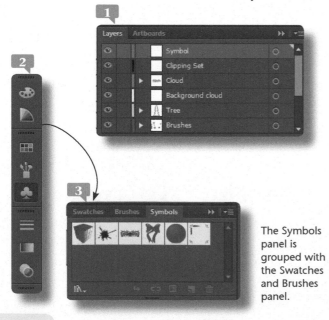

The Symbols panel is grouped with the Swatches and Brushes panel.

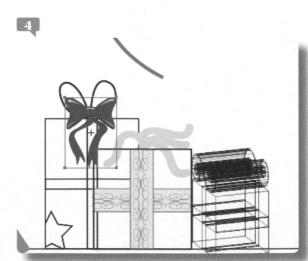

073

to place a symbol allows you to place it in an exact point in the illustration. If you use the **Place Symbol** command of the panel, the symbol is placed into the center of the artboard. Select any other available symbol and click on the button, which displays a curved arrow at the bottom of the panel.

5. The symbol appears in the center of the artboard. Once the symbol is placed, you can assign a name to the instance. To do this, and with the last instance selected, enter the desired name in the **Instance Name** field of the **Options Bar**.

6. The symbol instances can be manipulated freely without the fear of changing the original symbol. Click with the right mouse button on the last inserted instance, click on the **Transform** command of the context menu and select the **Scale** option.

7. In the **Scale** box, enter the value **40** in the **Scale** field of the **Uniform** section and click **OK** to confirm.

8. The instance has changed but not the symbol in the **Symbols** panel. Similarly, you can modify the symbol instances without the fear of damaging the original symbol (these instances can also be eliminated). With the instance selected, press the **Delete** key and check that the symbol appears in the panel.

Transform Again	Ctrl+D
Move...	Shift+Ctrl+M
Rotate...	
Reflect...	
Scale...	
Shear...	
Transform Each...	Alt+Shift+Ctrl+D
Reset Bounding Box	

Searching for symbols in the library

WHEN YOU OPEN THE SYMBOLS PANEL, Illustrator displays only six examples of the many symbols in the symbol library. The library is organized by topics and then in turn arranged alphabetically.

1. In this exercise, you will learn how to display the wide gallery of available symbols in Illustrator CS6 by accessing different libraries and how to add one of these symbols to the symbol panel. To do this, you will work on the illustration **Cover.ai** or **Cover2.ai**. So open it or put it in the foreground.

2. In this case, the **Symbols** panel displays only six predetermined symbols. To access the list of libraries, click on the first command at the bottom of this panel, the **Symbol Libraries Menu** icon.

3. The libraries are, as already discussed, arranged alphabetically in this menu. Depending on your needs, choose one. In this case, click on the **Maps** library.

4. In a new panel, which displays the name of the selected library, all symbols related to this topic are listed. If you want to include a symbol in the **Symbols** panel in order to use it

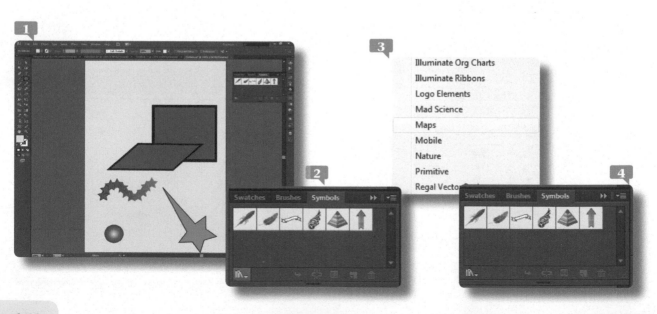

074

several times, you can click directly on the symbol, and it is automatically added to the panel. Click on the last symbol of the third row.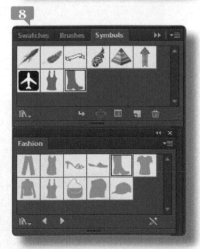

5. Once a library is open, you can see the other libraries from the same panel. To do this, you can display the Library menu or use the navigation buttons. You will have a look at both options. Click on the first command of the **Maps** panel and this time select the library called **Fashion**.

6. The new library replaces the previous one in the panel. Before displaying other libraries, click on a pair of symbols in this library to include them in the **Symbols** panel.

7. Click on the button that displays an arrow tip pointing to the right to display the next library in the panel.

8. Remember that the libraries are arranged alphabetically. This arrangement is also followed when you destroy them. Repeatedly press the same button to display the content of the other libraries.

9. Each library has a number of symbols that may not be displayed, to find these you can use the vertical scroll bar of the panel to display the bottom of the catalog.

10. Finish this exercise by clicking on the X button of the open library to close it.

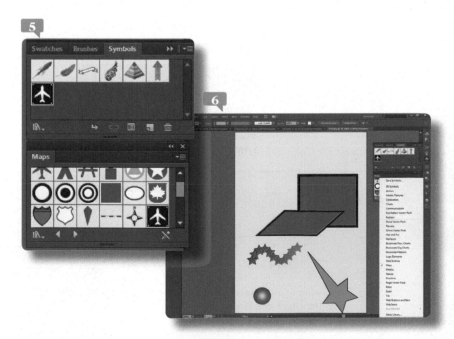

Editing and duplicating symbols

IMPORTANT

If you want to convert a text to a Flash symbol, you need to select the **MovieClip** option in the **Symbols Options** box. We will discuss this conversion later in this book.

DUPLICATING OR COPYING A SYMBOL in the Symbols panel is an easy way to create a new symbol based on an existing one. The process of duplication is extremely easy and is carried out from the panel.

1. In this exercise, you will continue to work with the Symbols panel. You will learn how to edit a symbol, access its options, and duplicate it to create a new one. In the **Symbols** panel, click the first of the symbols added in the previous exercise that displays an airplane. 🗨

2. Drag it three times within the central rectangle of the artwork. 🗨

3. In the **Options Bar**, click the **Edit symbol** button. 🗨

4. A dialog box appears in which the program warns you about editing the symbol definition. As indicated in this dialog box, it is important to bear in mind that the changes realized on the instance will be applied to all instances of this symbol in the document. Click on **OK** to continue. 🗨

5. The symbol is edited in the isolation mode. You will now

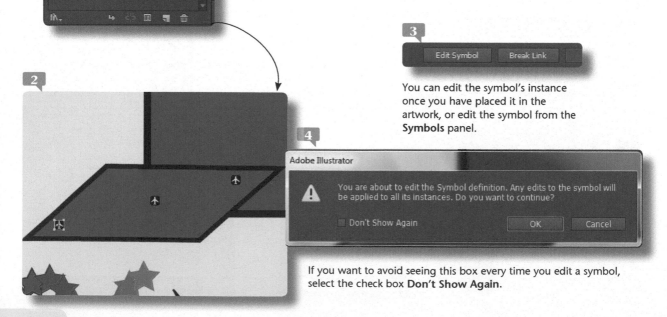

You can edit the symbol's instance once you have placed it in the artwork, or edit the symbol from the **Symbols** panel.

If you want to avoid seeing this box every time you edit a symbol, select the check box **Don't Show Again**.

modify its orientation. Select the symbol with a click and click on the **Transform** link in the **Options Bar**.

6. Enter the value **45** in the **Rotate** field at the bottom left of the panel and press **Return** to confirm the rotation.

7. Click on a free area of the artwork to check the orientation change.

8. You can now exit the isolation mode. To do this, click on the arrow that points to the left at the top of the window, next to the name of the symbol.

9. The change is immediately performed on all symbol instances in the artwork as well as in the **Symbols** panel. Select the modified symbol in the panel and click on the **Symbol Options** command, which is the fourth icon at the bottom of the panel.

10. In the **Symbol Options** dialog box, assign a new name to the symbol and click on **OK** to confirm.

11. You will now learn how to duplicate a symbol to edit it while keeping the original intact. Select another symbol, click on the menu command at the top right of the panel and select the **Duplicate Symbol** option.

Redefine Symbol
Duplicate Symbol
Delete Symbol
Edit Symbol

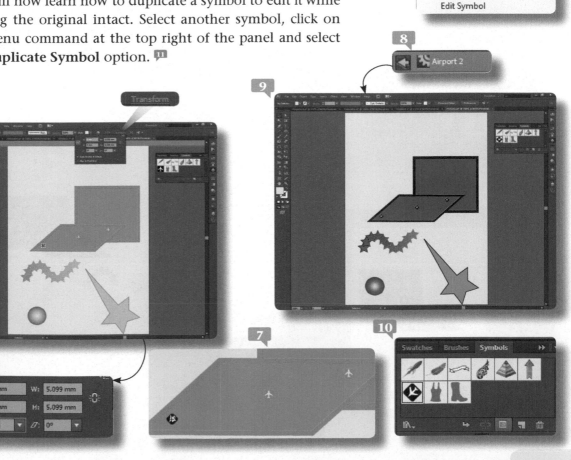

Expanding a symbol instance

EXPANDING A SYMBOL INSTANCE in Illustrator means separating the different elements from which it is made, usually a background and an object. Expanding a symbol is very simple and allows you to customize these elements in different ways.

1. In this exercise, you will learn how to expand a symbol instance to modify the different elements a symbol is made from. Click on the symbol that you have duplicated in the previous exercise, 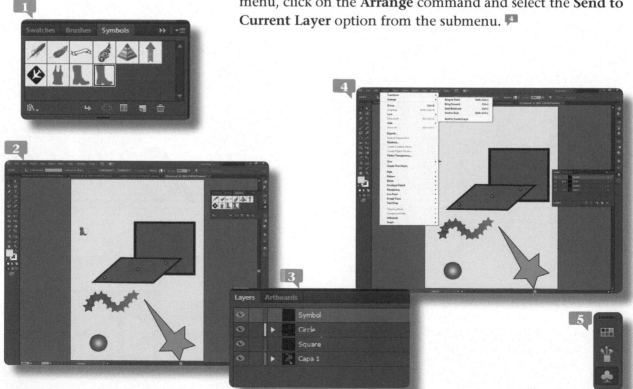 and drag it to place it in a free area of the artwork.

2. Before continuing, and to make it easier to manipulate objects in the illustration, create a new layer where you will place the symbol instance you are working with. Open the **Layers** panel, create a new layer and rename it **Symbol**.

3. Select the symbol instance in the illustration, open the **Object** menu, click on the **Arrange** command and select the **Send to Current Layer** option from the submenu.

4. Continue by displaying the **Symbols** panel again.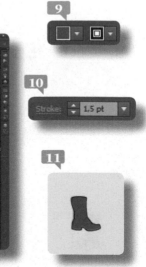

5. Select the symbol instance and click on the **Break Link to Symbol** command, which is displayed by a broken chain link at the bottom of the **Symbols** panel. 6

6. As you can see in the **Options Bar**, the program places the components of the symbol instance in a group. According to the modifications you want to perform, you can ungroup it to manipulate the fill and stroke separately. To do this, open the **Object** menu and click on the **Ungroup** command. 7

7. You will change the fill and apply a stroke. In the **Options Bar**, open the Fill field and select the color you prefer. 8

8. Open the **Stroke** field and select the color black from the Swatches panel. 9

9. Also increase the weight by selecting a value from the list in the **Options Bar** or by manually entering the desired value. 10

10. Click on a free area of the artwork to have a look at the changes realized on the symbol instance. 11

You can see that expanded symbol instances act as independent objects in the illustration. In the following exercise, you will learn how to create new symbols and how to replace symbol instances with other symbols.

076

IMPORTANT

In order to expand a symbol and manipulate it freely, you can also choose to display the Object menu and select the Expand command. It is the same effect as if you would use the **Break Link to Symbol** command of the Symbols panel.

Expand...

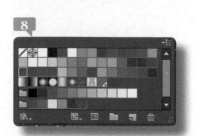

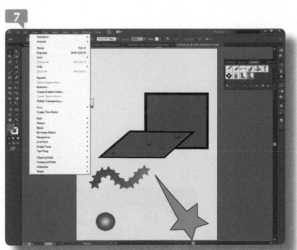

According to the modifications you want to perform on the expanded object, it will not be necessary to ungroup it.

Creating new symbols

IMPORTANT

The duplication of symbols and their subsequent modification with the help of the **isolation mode** is another way to create new symbols.

ILLUSTRATOR PROVIDES SEVERAL METHODS for creating new symbols. You can use the New Symbol command in the Symbols panel or duplicate existing symbols and modify them. In any case, you can expand the wide symbols library of the program by customizing objects and saving them as such.

1. In this exercise, you will learn how to create and add new symbols to the Symbols panel as well as to a symbols library. You start by eliminating one of the available symbols in the panel. Click on the icon and double-click on the **Delete Symbol** command, which is the last icon at the bottom of the **Symbols** panel.

2. In the confirmation box that appears, click on **Yes** to permanently delete the symbol.

3. The symbol disappears from the panel. Use the object that you modified in the previous exercise (you will continue to work with the file **Cover.ai** or **Cover2.ai**) to create a new symbol. Click on this object in the artwork.

4. Click on the **New symbol** button, the second to last icon at the bottom of the **Symbols** panel.

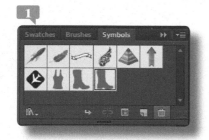

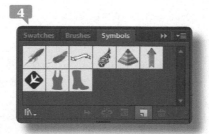

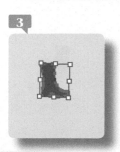

5. The **Symbol Options** dialog box appears, where you need to assign a name to the new item. In the **Name** field, type in a name you prefer to create it. **5**

6. The other options in this box are used to create dynamic Flash items. Later in this book we will discuss this feature in detail. Click on the **OK** button to create the new symbol.

7. The new symbol is displayed in the **Symbols** panel, which means that you can use it as often as we want. **6** Try it out by dragging the new symbol several times on to the picture. **7**

8. You will now learn how to replace symbols that are already placed in the artwork with other existing ones. With the help of the **Shift** key, select a pair of symbols from the previous step. **8**

9. In the **Options Bar**, display the **Replace** field (which displays the image of the selected symbol at this time) and choose another of the available symbols. **9**

10. The selected symbols have been replaced correctly. **10** We recommend that you discover the great possibilities of working with symbols. Before finishing this exercise, we want to show you how you can create a new symbol library. Select the symbols that interest you in the **Symbols** panel, display the menu of this panel and click on the **Save Symbol Library** command. **11**

11. Assign a name you prefer to the library and press **Save**.

IMPORTANT

It is important to know that you cannot add, delete, or edit items in symbol libraries. Symbol libraries created by the user are saved in the **Symbol Library** menu within the category called **User Defined**.

User Defined

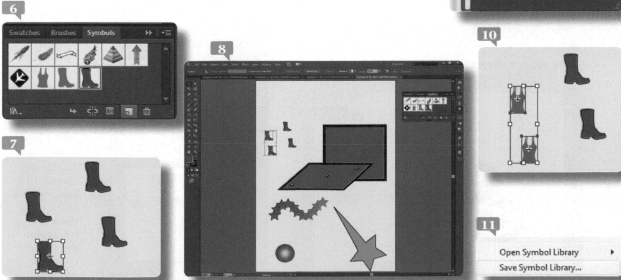

Creating symbol sets

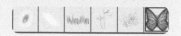
A SYMBOL SET IS A GROUP OF SYMBOL INSTANCES created with the Illustrator Symbol Sprayer tool. This tool acts like a particle sprayer and lets you add a large number of identical objects to the artboard at one time.

1. In this exercise, you will learn how to use the Symbol Sprayer Tool to create symbol sets. To do this, use the sample file **Tomato.ai**, which you can download from our website and copy it into your documents folder. Your goal is to draw a wild place with flowers and insects. Start by creating a new layer where you will place the symbol set. In the **Layers** panel, create a new layer and name it **Symbol Set**.

2. Display the **Symbols** panel, open the **Symbol Library** menu and click on the **Nature** option.

3. In this library, you will find all the symbols you need. Click on one of the grass symbols, which are included in the **Symbols** panel.

4. Select the symbol and activate the **Symbol Sprayer Tool** in the **Tools** panel. Click on the previously mentioned tool, which is displayed by an aerosol can icon.

5. By selecting this tool, the pointer adopts the shape of this

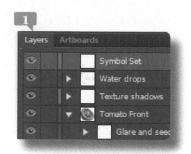

The Symbol Sprayer Tool icon contains all the tools needed to manipulate the inserted symbols in the artwork.

tool surrounded by a circle. This is the diameter of the brush. Before inserting the symbol set, you will modify this feature. Double-click on the **Symbol Sprayer Tool** in the **Tools** panel.

6. In the **Symbolism Tools Options** dialog box, enter the value **40mm** in the **Diameter** field and click on **OK** to accept it. 5

7. Then click on it and drag it to insert the symbol set. 6

8. You now have the first symbol set. From the **Nature** panel, this time choose a symbol of decorative plants, 7 select the **Symbol Sprayer Tool**, and click several times on the grass area. 8

9. Repeat the same with the sand symbol.

10. Choose from the library one of the insect symbols, for example a butterfly, and double-click on it to edit it in the **Symbols** panel.

11. Significantly reduce the size from the **Transform** panel 9 and exit the isolation mode.

12. Insert various symbols on the illustration with the **Symbol Sprayer Tool** 10 and finish this exercise by saving the changes.

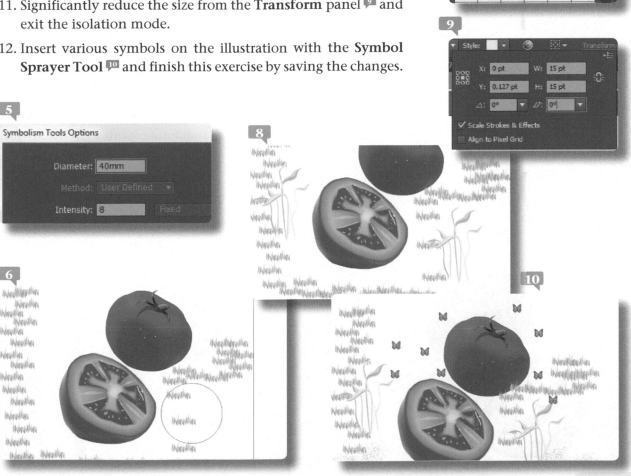

Editing symbol sets (I)

THE SYMBOL TOOL LETS YOU create and modify symbol instances in a set. After creating a symbol set with the Symbol Sprayer Tool, you can change the characteristics of the density, color, place, size, rotation, transparency, and style of all the instances in the set.

1. In this exercise, you will learn how to edit and modify the symbol set that you created in the previous exercise. The first thing you want to check is if the entire set is selected when you click on any of the symbol instances that make up the set. Click on one of these instances with the **Selection Tool**.

2. The symbol set that contains the insect (the butterfly) is independent from the rest as you have modified the original symbol. Check it by clicking on one of these instances.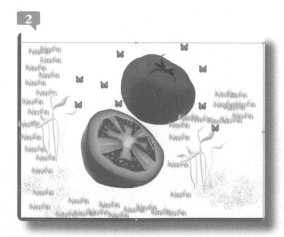

3. You will remove the independent set and add multiple instances of the same symbol to the existing set. Select the set and press the **Delete** key.

4. Check if the symbol is still in the **Symbols** panel. Then select, with the **Selection Tool**, all remaining symbols in the artwork and click on the **Symbol Sprayer Tool**.

079

5. Select the butterfly (or insect) symbol in the **Symbols** panel and click on the area of the symbol set where you want to place the new instances.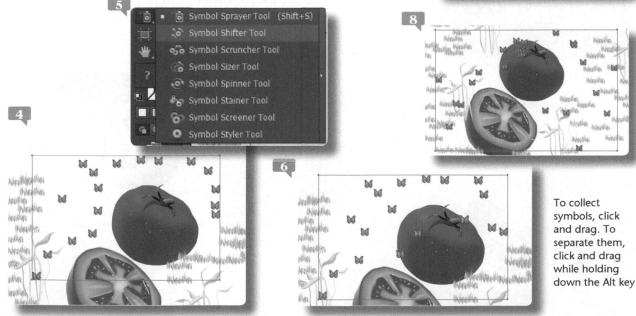

6. The instances of a symbol set display a stacking order when they were added to this set. However, once the set is created, you can easily modify this order. Place the grass instances in the first place. To do this, select the symbol corresponding to these instances in the **Symbols** panel.

7. Then open the **Symbol Sprayer Tool** in the **Tools** panel, and click on the **Symbol Shifter Tool**.

8. To bring the symbol instances forward, hold down the **Shift** key and click on each instance.

9. You will also move the instances within the set. Select the same tool, click on some of the instances and drag them down.

10. Another interesting symbolism tool is called the **Symbol Scruncher Tool**. With the help of this tool, you can zoom in and out the symbol instances. Try it out with the symbol instances of the insect. Select the symbol in the **Symbols** panel and select the mentioned tool in the Symbol Tool group.

11. Click on the area where you want to approach the instances of the selected symbol.

To collect symbols, click and drag. To separate them, click and drag while holding down the Alt key

Editing symbol sets (II)

AS AREADY SHOWN IN THE PREVIOUS EXERCISE, creating symbol sets achieves realistic drawings. The subsequent manipulation of the sets allows you to adjust the instances to get more accurate results.

1. In this second exercise dedicated to the symbolism tools, you will continue practicing with the group of symbols added in previous exercises. In the last exercise, you saw how to remove symbol sets, how to add instances to a set, move them, and gather them. You will now reduce the size of a decorative plant. To do this, selct the set and click on the corresponding symbol in the **Symbols** panel.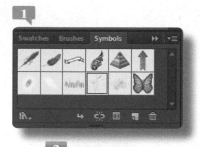

2. Display the icon for the **Symbol Tool** in the **Tools** panel and click on **Symbol Sizer.**

3. Press the **Alt** key and without releasing it click several times on one of the plants to reduce its size.

4. The next tool we will show you is the one that allows you to change the direction of the symbol instances in a set. In this case, click on the symbol of the insect in the **Symbols** panel and select the **Symbol Spinner Tool** in the **Tools** panel.

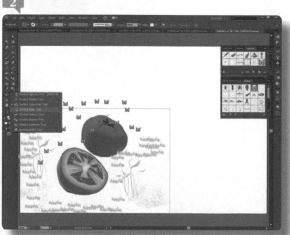

If you want to increase the size of an instance, proceed without clicking on the Alt key.

080

5. To change the direction of the butterflies, click on the instance you want to modify, and without releasing the mouse button drag it until it turns in the direction you want. 5

6. You already know that the symbols display a number of default characteristics, among which you can find the color feature. With the **Symbol Stainer Tool** you can modify this color by changing the hue toward the tint color. In the **Color** panel, choose the fill color you want to apply to the instance. 6

7. Select the **Symbol Stainer Tool** in the **Symbol Tool** group of the **Tools** panel.

8. Click on the symbol instances you want to stain with the selected color. 7

9. The amount of colorization gradually increases and the color of the symbol instance changes little by little to the chosen color. Be aware that the **Symbol Stainer Tool** has a disadvantage: it increases the file size and therefore decreases preformance. If you are planning to use a Flash illustration, you should not use it. As a last modification, you will increase the transparency of one of your instances. In order to do this, select the **Symbol Screener Tool** in the **Tools** panel 8 and click on the instances where you want to apply the transparency. 9

IMPORTANT

You already know that you can adjust the diameter of the Symbol tool from the **Symbol Tool Options** box, which you can access by double-clicking on the Symbol Tool in the **Tools** panel. Select a small diameter to modify small instances, and vice versa.

Diameter: 30 pt

Method: User Defined

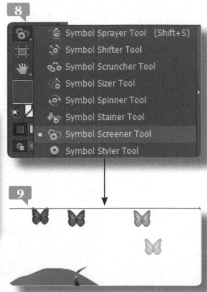

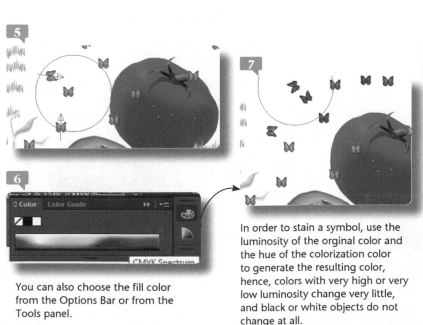

You can also choose the fill color from the Options Bar or from the Tools panel.

In order to stain a symbol, use the luminosity of the orginal color and the hue of the colorization color to generate the resulting color, hence, colors with very high or very low luminosity change very little, and black or white objects do not change at all.

If you want to reduce transparency instead of increasing it, press the Alt key while clicking on the symbol instances.

Adding and modifying flares

ILLUSTRATOR PROVIDES A UNIQUE TOOL to create flare objects with a bright center, a halo, rays, and rings: the Flare Tool. Flares include a center handle and an end handle; the center handle is in the bright center of the flare—the flare path begins from this point.

1. In this exercise, you will get to know the **Flare Tool**, which we use to give an element of uniqueness to the illustration **Tomato.ai.** You will create a flare with the properties that the program establishes and draw another completely customized one. Click on the arrow tip of the **Rectangle Tool** in the **Tools** panel, and select the **Flare Tool** from the list. 🗨1

2. Press the **Alt** key and, without releasing it, click on the whole tomato in the artwork to add a default flare. 🗨2 Click anywhere outside of the selection to have a look at the final result. 🗨3

3. The flare is inserted into the picture with specific dimensions and characteristics. You will undo the creation of the flare to draw a new one with customized characteristics. Display the **Edit** menu and click on the **Undo Flare** command. 🗨4

4. Access the **Flare Tool Options** box to set different compo-

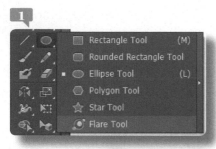

The point where you click after selecting the **Flare Tool** will be the point where the center handle of the object will be placed.

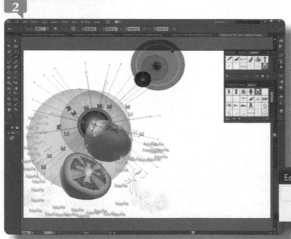

081

nents of the object from there. To do this, double-click on that tool. **5**

5. The **Flare Tool Options** box is divided into four sections, one for each of the flare components. Start by adjusting the center. In the **Diameter** field, enter the value **30 pt.** **6**

6. Modify the opacity or the degree of transparency and brightness as you prefer, and enter percentages in the corresponding fields. **7**

7. Move on to the halo. In the **Growth** field of the **Halo** section, set a percentage of 10% of the overall size and keep the default tolerance of the halo. **8**

8. As for the rays, you will reduce the number that appears by default. In the **Number** field of the **Rays** section, enter or find the value **7.**

9. The **Longest** field allows you to set the percentage that represents the longest ray in relation to the average ray. Enter the value **200%** in this field and keep the default tolerance. **9**

10. Click on the **Rings** option check box to disable it and press **OK** to apply the changes.

11. In order to draw the flare, click on the point of the artwork where you want to add it and click on **OK** to close the Options box. **10**

12. Select the **Selection Tool**, click on a free area of the artwork to deselect the flare **11** and save the changes.

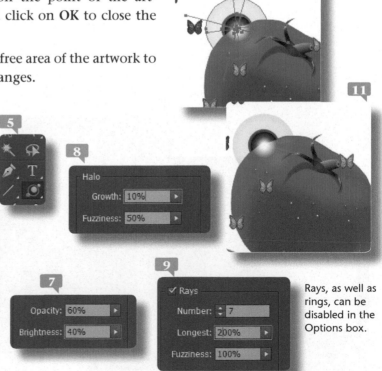

Rays, as well as rings, can be disabled in the Options box.

Importing a bitmap image

BITMAP IMAGES, TECHNICALLY CALLED raster images, use a rectangular grid of picture elements (pixels) to represent images. When working with this type of image in Illustrator, you edit pixels rather than objects or shapes.

1. In this first exercise dedicated to the use of images in Illustrator, you will learn about what you need to keep in mind when importing these files into the program. In this exercise, you will use a new illustration in white and a file that can be downloaded from our website called **Butterfly.bmp**. (Alternatively, you can use any other images of this type that are stored on your computer.) Open the **File** menu and click on the **New** command. [1]

2. In the **New Document** dialog box, type the word **Image** in the **Name** field, keep the other options as they are, and press the **OK** button. [2]

3. The **Place** command is the main import method, as it provides the highest level of compatibility for the file formats, the placement options, and the color. Reopen the **File** menu and click on that command. [3]

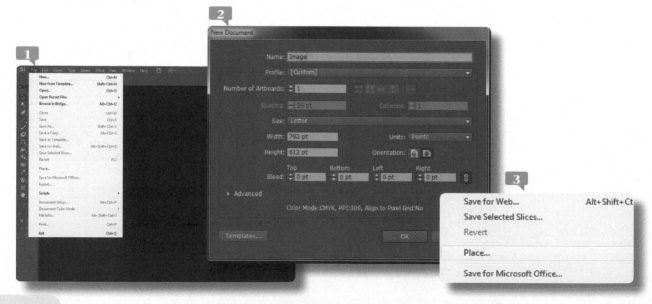

4. Find and select **Butterfly.bmp** (or any other file you want to place) in the **Place** dialog box, disable the **Link** option and press the **Place** button.

5. The image file is embedded in the artwork, which means that it displays its full resolution and is a separate object of the illustration.  The **Links** panel allows you to manage the embedded and linked files. Open this panel displaying the **Window** menu and select the **Links** command.

6. The **Links** panel displays the file name next to the miniature and to the right the symbol that indicates that it is embedded. Import the same file again but this time linked. Open the **File** menu and click on the **Place** command.

7. In the **Place** dialog box, locate and use the same file as before and then click on the **Link** option.

8. Press the **Place** button to insert the new file into the illustration.

9. The linked file is located in the center of the document positioned on top of the previous one, and its name also appears in the **Links** panel. Make sure that no symbol appears along with the name as this would mean that it is still not embedded. Move the new image using the **Selection Tool** until both images are displayed in the artwork.

082

IMPORTANT

Linked artwork can be modified using transformatin tools and effects; however, it is not possible to select and edit individual components in the artwork as it is the case in embedded artwork.

Linked File   Mariposa.bmp

Manipulating linked or embedded files

APART FROM THE OBVIOUSLY INCREASED SIZE of the illustration, the difference between working with linked or embedded files depends on the use and manipulation of the image. In the case of linked images, the editing of the original and its automatic update in Illustrator is an advantage for modifying images.

1. In this exercise, you will learn about some of the differences between working with linked or embedded images. Start by selecting the linked image in the **Links** panel and clicking on the **Go to Link** command, which is the second icon at the bottom of the panel. (Note that these files do not display any symbol in the panel, unlike embedded files.) **1**

2. This way, you can select the image you prefer without any problems. **2** See that the words **Linked File** are displayed in orange in the **Options Bar**, which serves as a connection that opens the **Links** panel. The link with the file name to the right displays an options menu related to the image. Click on that link. **3**

3. The opening menu displays a number of options related to the original image. Click on the **Link Information** option.

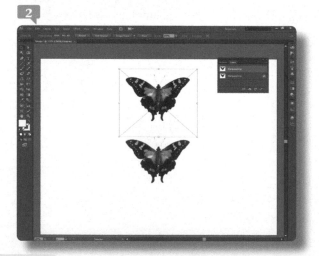

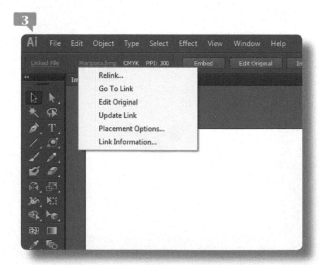

083

4. The **Link Information** dialog box displays all data related to the original file. Press the **OK** button.

5. The **Options Bar** contains the commands to embed the linked image and to edit the original. This option is very useful to modify the image with tools that are not available in Illustrator. Press the **Edit Original** button.

6. The image is opened in Photoshop. You will modify the color mode to a grayscale image. Display the **Image** menu, click on the **Mode** command and select from the submenu the **Grayscale** option by clicking on **Discard** in the appearing dialog box.

7. Close Photoshop after saving the changes and return to Illustrator.

8. Check that the linked image is still in color. You now have to update the link. To do this, click on the file name link in the **Options Bar** and select the **Update link** command from the menu.

9. The image immediately appears in black and white, which means it has been updated successfully. We will now show you how an embedded image does not have any original link: click on the embedded image in color.

10. The **Edit Original** button as well as the **Embed** button are disabled in the **Options Bar**. Click on a free area of the artwork to remove the selection of the image and finish this exercise.

IMPORTANT

If you are editing an original image and the performed changes don't update the link immediately, Illustrator detects that the image has not been updated and sends a warning message. You can click on **Yes** and the update will be carried out automatically, but you can also cancel this message and take care of it later.

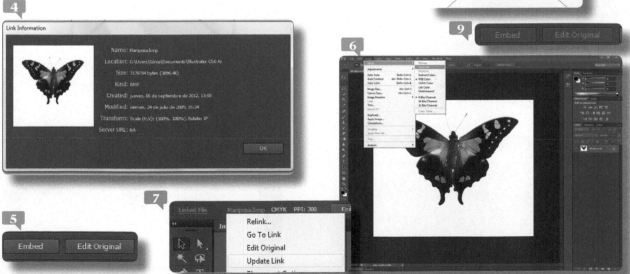

Importing Photoshop images

ILLUSTRATOR ALLOWS YOU TO WORK WITH ARTWORK from Photoshop PSD files, with all their advantages. Illustrator supports most Photoshop data, including layer comps, layers, editable text, and paths. This means that you can transfer files between Photoshop and Illustrator without losing the ability to edit the artwork later.

1. In this exercise, you will learn how to import a PSD file format (that is, realized with Photoshop) into Illustrator. If you have any files in this format, you can use them to carry out this exercise, if not, you can download **Giraffes.psd** from our website and save the file to your computer. Before importing the file, create a new layer. Display the **Layers** panel and create a new layer called **Giraffes.**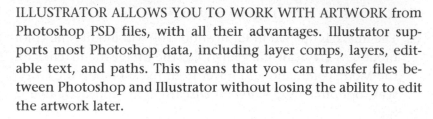

2. You will create a second layer where you will place one of the two images included in the previous exercises. Create a new layer and rename it **Image Color.**

3. Select the embedded image and the **Image Color** layer, open the **Object** menu, click on the **Arrange** command and select the **Send to Current Layer** option from the submenu.

Remember that the objects are added to the artwork according to the layer stacking order in the **Layers** panel. You can change this order by dragging the layers.

4. This way you have all the artwork objects organized in layers. Now select the **Giraffes** layer.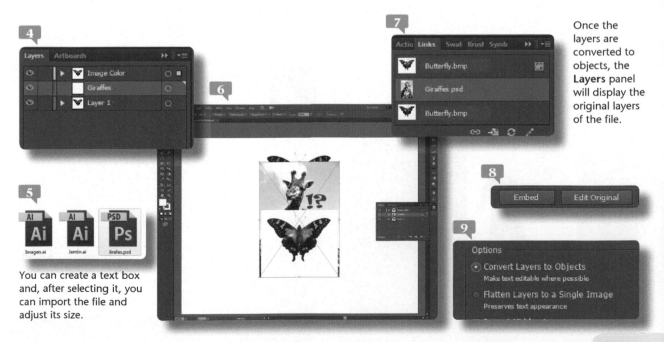

5. To import a Photoshop image, you need to proceed as with any other image type. Open the **File** menu and click on the **Place** command.

6. In the **Place** dialog box, locate the PSD file and press the **Place** button to import it into Illustrator.

7. As you can see in the **Options Bar**, files in Photoshop format are, by default, imported as linked rather than embedded, like bitmaps, for example. Open the **Links** panel to verify that the image also appears in the panel.

8. Reposition the three images by dragging them so they do not overlap and display the **Giraffes** image.

9. You will embed the image in your artwork (remember that you can subsequently unembed it without any problems). Click on the **Embed** button in the **Options Bar**.

10. The **Photoshop Import Options** box opens, in which you can configure the behavior of the layer. Originally, your sample file **Giraffes** had two layers, one of them containing text. In the **Options** section, select the **Convert Layers to Objects** option and click on **OK** to embed the file in the artwork.

11. Save the changes.

084

IMPORTANT

When converting Photoshop layers to objects and to make text editable where possible (an option available in the Photoshop Import Options box), they preserve as much layer structure and text editability as possible without sacrificing appearance. However, keep in mind that the file includes features that Illustrator does not support, it preserves the appearance of the artwork by merging and rasterizing the layers.

Once the layers are converted to objects, the **Layers** panel will display the original layers of the file.

You can create a text box and, after selecting it, you can import the file and adjust its size.

181

Moving paths from Photoshop to Illustrator

THE PATHS TO ILLUSTRATOR FUNCTION, which is included in the Export command of the File menu, enables you to export paths created in a Photoshop document to an Illustrator document. Paths can be created manually with the Pen Tool or they can be obtained from a selection. After exporting the path to Illustrator, you can usually manipulate it in this application.

1. To learn how to export paths from Photoshop to Illustrator, you will use the **Silhouette.jpg** file, which as always can be downloaded from our website and copied to your images folder. Once you have the file open in Photoshop, select the **Magic Wand Tool** and click on the Silhouette to select it.

2. You will now convert the selected shape to a path in Photoshop. To do this, click with the right mouse button on the selection and select the **Make Work Path** option in the appearing contextual menu.

3. Keep the tolerance value that appears by default in the **Create Work Path** box and click on **OK**.

4. To verify that the temporary work path is successfully created, activate the **Paths** panel.

5. You will now change the name of the work path. Double-click on it in the **Paths** panel, type the word **Silhouette** in the **Save Path** box and press the **OK** button. [4]

6. Once you have created the work path that you want to place in Illustrator, open the **File** menu, click on the **Export** option and select **Paths to Illustrator**. [5]

7. Select the **Silhouette** paths in the **Export Paths to File** box and press the **OK** button. [6]

8. Also assign the name **Silhouette** to the new Illustrator file that will be created and save it in your images folder.

9. Place Illustrator in the foreground, access the **Open** box by pressing the key combination **Ctrl + O**, locate and select the Illustrator file you have just exported and click on the **Open** button.

10. Keep the default options displayed in the **Convert to Artboards** box and press the **OK** button. [7]

11. Although the document is apparently blank, you can observe that its path has been exported correctly if you move the mouse cursor across the canvas. (Adjust the zoom display if necessary). When the path gets visible, select it, and click on any of the swatches of the **Color** panel to fill it with a color. [8]

12. To finish the exercise, close the **Silhouette** document and save the changes you have carried out.

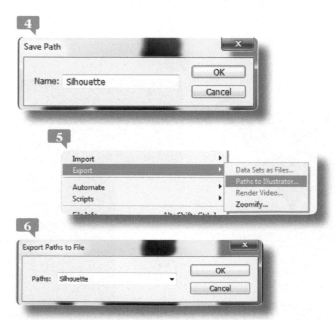

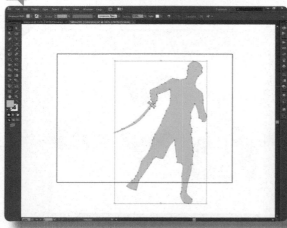

Converting an image to an editable vector

THE NEW LIVE TRACE COMMAND IN ILLUSTRATOR CS6 allows you to create new drawings based on an artwork or an existing image in a much simpler way than in earlier versions, thus achieving a much sharper result with less need for retouching.

1. In this exercise, you will learn how to convert an image to an editable drawing in Illustrator CS6 using its powerful new image tracing engine. To do this, you will use the **Image Trace** command in the **Options Bar**, which appears when you select an image. Start by selecting the embedded image of the butterfly, located in the **Image Color** layer. 🔲

2. To trace the image using the default tracing options, click on the **Image Trace** button in the **Options Bar**. 🔲

3. After a quick automatic process, the image converts to a black and white drawing. 🔲 In this case you have used the default option (a black and white logo). Now look at one of the other options that is available.

4. In order to see more options, press **Ctrl + Z** to undo the trace, select the image, open the **Tracing Presets** menu, and have a look at the different options available. 🔲

You can also display the Object menu by clicking on the **Image Trace** command and selecting Create.

5. Click on **Low Fidelity Photo,** to obtain the following result. Press **Ctrl + Z** to undo the action and to continue practicing.

6. Let's use another example. Click on **Line Art** and have a look at the result. Press the key combination **Ctrl + Z** and this time trace again with the default option.

7. A tracing object is made up of two components: the original source image and the tracing result (which is the vector artwork). By default, only the tracing result is visible. However, you can change the display of both the original image and tracing results to best suit your needs. To do this, click on the arrow next to the **Tracing Result** option in the **Toolbar** to open the **Display Options.**

8. For example, have a look at the result of selecting the **Outlines** option. Select the **Tracing Result** option again.

9. By default, the tracing objects appear in the **Layers** panel with the name **Tracing Image.** Display this panel and click on the arrow tip of the **Image Color** layer.

10. All these options, which you have modified by using different panels, are also unified in the **Image Trace** panel, to the left of the display options in the **Toolbar.**

As you will see in later exercises, the images obtained by tracing can be edited and modified to adapt perfectly to your needs.

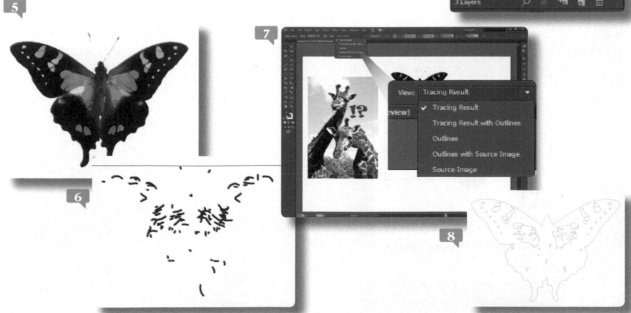

Modifying the result of a live trace

AFTER CREATING A TRACE OBJECT, Illustrator CS6 allows you to adjust the result at any time. By selecting the trace object, the Options Bar displays some adjustable parameters, although these can all be accessed by opening the Trace Options box.

1. In this exercise, you will adjust the result of the live trace that you performed on an image in the previous exercise. (A copy of the example file **Image.ai** can be found in the download area of our website.) Click on the tracing object to select it.

2. You can change the preset (or tracing type), the threshold (the value used to separate black from white) and the minimum area (the smallest detail, in pixels, which can be traced) from the **Options Bar**. Illustrator provides a tracing options box that you will access later. In the **Options Bar**, click on the **Image Trace Panel** command next to the **Preset** field.

3. In the **Tracing Options** box activate the **Preview** option to check the changes you'll make.

4. Display the **Advanced** tab to access more tracing options.

5. The default image trace is carried out in black and white. Have a look at the remaining available types. Illustrator contains 12 tracing types, besides the default trace. You will choose one as a swatch, but we recommend that you try out the aspect of the remaining types on your own. Open the **Mode** field of the **Presets** section and select the **Color** option.

6. Move the cursor of the **Paths** section to a high value (95%) for better adjustment of the image paths. ⑤

7. Have a look at the changes on the tracing object of the artwork. ⑥ If you activate the **Preview** option the changes are carried out immediately, so you do not need to press the **Trace** button when finished. At the top of the menu are some icons displaying different types of preset colors. Activating each type also activates different options. ⑦

8. In previous versions of Illustrator, you could find more options for modifying the traced image such as **Blur** or **Resample**. Due to the improvement of the tool in this version, the editing has been simplified and all variations can be realized from the tracing and image panel itself.

087

To let Illustrator determine the colors in the tracing, select **Default** in the Panel of the Tracing Options box field. If you prefer to use a custom palette for the tracing, select a name from the given options.

Tracings and Live Paint groups

AFTER CREATING A TRACE OBJECT, Illustrator allows you to convert it to a path or to a Live Paint group. This means that you can work with the layer as you would do with any other vector artwork.

1. In this exercise, you will learn how to convert the trace object created in the previous exercise to a Live Paint group. Select the image of the butterfly converted to a drawing. **1**

2. To convert the object to a Live Paint group, open the **Object** menu, click on **Image Trace** and select the **Expand** option. **2**

3. The **Expand** option allows to convert the trace object selected to a path. Note that when you perform this conversion, the object appears grouped. Open the **Object** menu again, this time select the **Live Paint** option and click on the **Make** option. **3**

4. The conversion is performed within seconds. Upon completion, the selected object displays all the parts it consists of. **4** Remember that you can now modify each path and each fill color separately. Try it out: enable the **Live Paint Bucket Tool** in the **Tools** panel. **5**

5. Open the **Fill** field in the **Options Bar** and click on a color you prefer.

6. Point the cursor on the paint group and when the area that you want to color is highlighted, click on it.

7. Remember that when you place the pointer over the path of the figure, you can also paint the outline of the object. Use the **Selection Tool** to click on an empty zone to have a better look at the result.

8. You will now learn, as an example, how to convert a trace object to a path. Since you do not have any more objects of this type, you will trace the black and white image to convert it later to a path. Choose the image and then click on the **Image Trace** button in the **Options Bar**.

9. The trace was carried out using the default settings. Click on the **Expand** button in the same **Options Bar** to convert the new trace object to a path.

10. The conversion is also carried out instantly. Now you can work with the components of the traced artwork as if they were individual objects. Click on a free area of the artwork to undo the selection and save the changes to finish the exercise.

088

Rasterizing a drawing

RASTERIZATION IS THE PROCESS BY WHICH a vector graphic changes to a bitmap image. During the process, Illustrator converts the graphic's paths into pixels. The rasterization options you set determine the size and other characteristics of the resulting pixels.

1. In this exercise, you will learn how to change a drawing to a bitmap image, that is, to rasterize it. Therefore, you will practice with the example illustration **Tomatoes2.ai**, which is the modified version of the **Tomatoes** file that you can download from our website. Once you have copied this file, open it in Illustrator.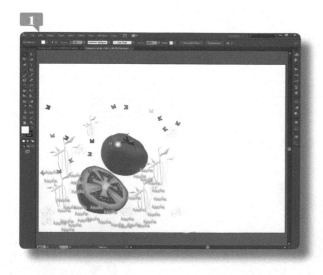

2. You have created a symbol set consisting of various grass, insect, and flower symbols in this illustration. You will convert this set to an image. First, you will select the set of elements with the **Selection Tool**.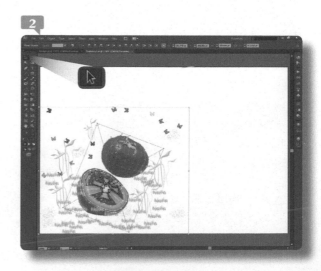

3. Rasterization can be performed in two different ways, depending on the result you want to achieve: if you use the **Rasterize** command in the **Object** menu, the conversion will be carried out continuously, whereas if you choose to apply

the **Rasterize** effect in the **Effect** menu, the rasterization will be created without changing the underlying structure of the selected object. Since in this case you want to keep the original appearance, open the **Effect** menu and click on the **Rasterize** command.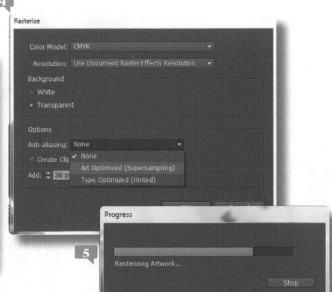

4. Indicate the conversion options in the **Rasterize** dialog box. Keep the **CMYK** option in the **Color Model** field selected to obtain a color image. In the **Resolution** section click on **Use Document Raster Effects Resolution** to use global resolution settings.

5. The **Background** section determines the conversion of the transparent areas of a vector graphic to pixels. By default, the **Transparent** option is checked, with the help of which you can create an alpha channel. Open the **Anti-aliasing** field in the **Options** section and select **Art Optimized**.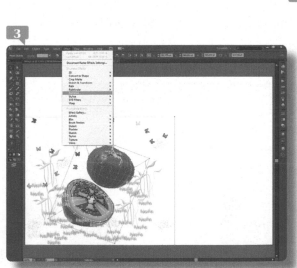

6. The **Create Clipping Mask** option creates a mask that makes the background of the rasterized image appear transparent. Since you have indicated that you will create a transparent background, we do not need to check this option. Finally, the option **Add [] Around Object** adds a border around the rasterized image, using the specified number of pixels. With the help of this border you can achieve a snapshot effect. Keep the value that appears by default and press **OK** to rasterize the drawing.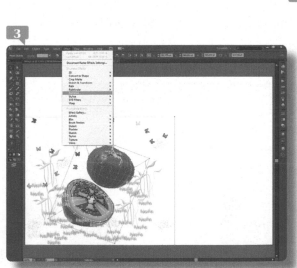

IMPORTANT

If an effect looks good on-screen, but loses detail or appears jagged when printed, increase the document rasterizing effects resolution.

✓ Screen (72 ppi)
   Medium (150 ppi)
   High (300 ppi)
   Use Document Raster Effects Resolution

   Other

If you select the **Rasterize** command in the **Object** menu, you can also access the **Rasterize Options** box.

Applying a raster effect

IMPORTANT

Since the adjustments have a great influence on the artistic result, it is important to check the settings of the document raster effects before you start working with the effects. To access the Rasterization settings box, open the **Effect** menu and click on the **Document Raster Effects Settings** command.

Document Raster Effects Settings...

RASTER EFFECTS GENERATE PIXELS RATHER than vector data. When you apply a raster effect, Illustrator is basing it on the Document raster effect settings to determine the resolution of the resulting image. In this version, these effects have been improved to provide the best appearance in different media regardless of the resolution configuration.

1. In this exercise, you will work on the drawing that you converted to bitmaps in the previous exercise, which is to say, on the rasterized drawing of the artwork **Tomatoes2.ai**. To begin, select the drawing. ▣

2. Effects based on rasters include the **SVG Filters** command, all effects at the bottom of the **Effect** menu, and the **Drop Shadow**, **Inner Glow**, **Outer Glow**, and **Feather** commands of the **Stylize** submenu. Look at some of the effects that are produced on the image. Open the **Effect** menu and click on the **SVG Filters** option. ▣

3. SVG effects are a set of XML properties that describe various mathematical operations. Illustrator provides a standard set of SVG effects. You can use the effects with their default properties, edit the XML code to produce custom effects, or write new SVG effects. In this case, click on the **AI_CoolBreeze** effect. ▣

Note that some of these effects can be memory-intensive, especially when applied to a high-resolution bitmap image.

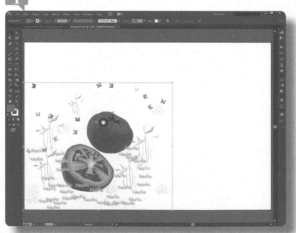

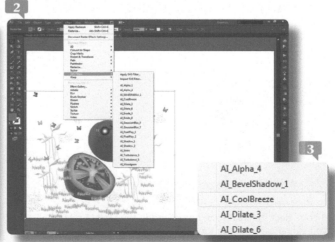

4. The effect is applied after a brief raster progress. Since you want to display other effects, you will undo this action. Press the key combination **Ctrl + Z** to get back to the original image.

5. Reopen the **Effect** menu, click on the **SVG Filters** command and this time select the **AI_Turbulence 3** effect.

6. Have a look at the artistic result you have obtained. As already mentioned, these filters are applied with a number of default parameters, but Illustrator allows you to edit them in XML to carry out the changes you consider appropriate. See how: open the **Appearance** panel and click on the last applied effect.

7. In the **Apply SVG filter** box, click on the **Edit SVG filter** command that is displayed by the letters **fx**.

8. This is the edited filter in the XML language. If you know this language, you can customize the effect from this code. As this is not your task, press the **Cancel** button in the two open boxes.

9. Press the key combination **Ctrl + Z** again to undo the effect.

10. In order to finish, you will apply another effect type that is not included in the SVG filter category. Open the **Effect** menu, click on the **Stylize** command and select the **Drop Shadow** effect.

11. Keep the default options in the **Drop Shadow** box and click on **OK** to apply the effect.

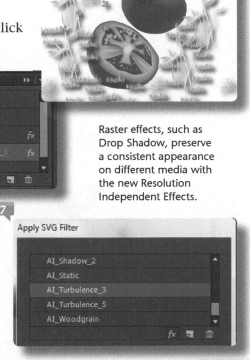

Raster effects, such as Drop Shadow, preserve a consistent appearance on different media with the new Resolution Independent Effects.

Using artistic effects

ARTISTIC EFFECTS SIMULATE A PAINTERLY appearance on traditional media. Such effects are raster-based and use the document's raster effects settings whenever you apply the effect to a vector object.

1. In this second exercise dedicated to raster effects, you will practice with the so-called artistic effects. Therefore, you will use the document **Image.ai** again. Open it or put it in the foreground.

2. You will work on the butterfly image that you have converted to a path in previous exercises. To do this, you will convert it again to an image. Select the drawing with the **Selection Tool**, open the **Object** menu and click on the **Rasterize** effect.

3. In the **Rasterize** dialog box, keep all options as they appear by default and click on **OK**.

4. You can now start applying some of the available artistic effects. Open the **Effect** menu and click on the **Artistic** command.

5. As you can see, Illustrator contains fifteen so-called artistic effects. Select the **Sponge** effect.

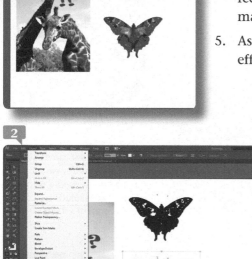

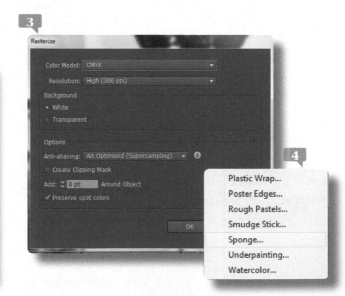

6. The **Sponge** window opens displaying the preview of the effect on the image on the left. Reduce the percentage of the preview to see it entirely. Open the display field at the bottom left of the window and click on **Fit on Screen**. 5

7. In the center panel of this window you can find the categories of the effect, displaying, in this case, the content of the **Artistic** category. This way you can try out other effects before applying any of them permanently. Click on the **Underpainting** effect in the center panel. 6

8. Select the **Plastic Wrap** effect and have a look at the result. 7

9. Each effect features its Properties panel on the right side of the window. These properties can be modified to obtain the look that it suits best. In the case of the Plastic Wrap effect, you can change the intensity, detail, and smoothing. Modify these parameters 8 according to your taste and click on **OK** to apply the effect on the image of the artwork.

10. After applying the effect, you can access the Properties box again from the **Appearance** panel. Display this panel and click on the last applied effect. 9

11. From this box you can change the effect or modify the properties of the current effect. Click on **Cancel** to exit the box without saving any modifications.

7

8

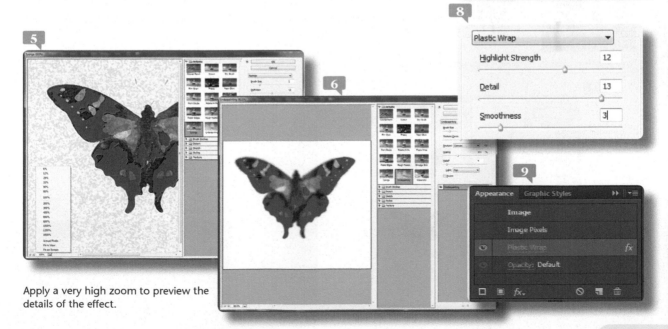

Apply a very high zoom to preview the details of the effect.

Applying Gaussian Blur and other effects

IN THE NEW VERSION OF ILLUSTRATOR, the effects of the Blur command in the Effect menu have improved spectacularly. Blur effects give a very realistic touch to the images in Illustrator CS6. You can now apply them much faster and with better results.

1. In this exercise, you will continue practicing with the effects available in Illustrator. This time, you will work on the **Giraffes** image, which is included in the document **Image.ai**, but if you prefer, you can practice on any other bitmap image you have saved on your computer. To begin, select the mentioned image.

2. Apply a Gaussian Blur. This effect type blurs a selection by an adjustable amount, removes high-frequency detail, and can produce a hazy effect. Open the **Effect** menu, click on the **Blur** command and select the **Gaussian Blur** effect.

3. Before applying the effect, the **Gaussian Blur** box opens in which the only configurable parameter is the radius in pixels you want to blur. In this new version of Illustrator CS6, the preview is carried out directly on the original image, making the process significantly easier. Then, if required, adjust the blur radius in the appropriate field by entering the value you

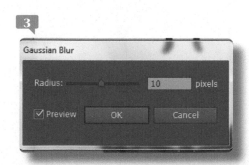

prefer or by using the control bar. When finished, click on **OK** to apply the blur.

4. Have a look at the effect on the image. 🔁 Now you will undo the action again to try out the remaining blur effects. Press the key combination **Ctrl + Z**.

5. You will now apply a Radial Blur. Therefore, open the **Effect** menu, click on the **Blur** command and this time select **Radial Blur**.

6. The **Radial Blur** box opens where you can set up the method (by rotation or zooming) and the quality, apart from the amount of blur. 🔁 Keep the default settings or modify them according to your taste and click on **OK** to apply the new blur.🔁

7. In order to apply the third blur, you will use a different procedure to avoid repeating what you have seen so far. Press the key combination **Ctrl + Z**.

8. Open the **Appearance** panel and click on the **Add new effect** icon, which is displayed by the letters fx at the bottom of the panel. 🔁

9. The opening menu contains the same commands as the Effect menu. Click on the **Blur** command and this time select the **Smart Blur** option.

10. Modify the parameters of this effect as you wish and click on **OK** to apply the new blur. 🔁

In the **Blur Center** graph, mark the point where the spin for the blur should originate.

Adding a brush stroke effect

THE SO-CALLED BRUSH STROKE EFFECTS create a painterly or fine arts look in images placed in Illustrator by using different brush and ink strokes.

1. In order to practice with the brush stroke effects, you will use a new image: **Panda.bmp**, which you can download from our website. Remember that you can use any other image in bmp format that you have saved on your computer.) Place the image in an area free of the artwork, open the **File** menu and select the **Place** command.  (Remember to embed the image from the **Options Bar**.)

2. Open the **Effect** menu and click on the **Brush Strokes** command.

3. Illustrator features eight different stroke effects. As in the case of the artistic effects in previous exercises, you will apply some of these available effects. We recommend trying out the remaining effects on your own. Click on the **Crosshatch** effect.

4. The **Crosshatch** window opens and displays a preview of the image with the applied effect. The major advantage of this box is (as we have seen in the previous exercise) that you can

093

have a look at the appearance of all effects before choosing one of them. In this case, keep the default stroke length options, sharpness, and intensity, then click on **OK** to apply it.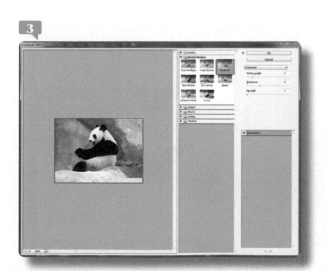

5. The **Crosshatch** effect preserves the details and features of the original image while adding texture and roughening the edges of the colored areas in the image with simulated pencil hatching. You will discard this effect and apply another one available. Press the key combination **Ctrl + Z**.

6. This time, open the **Appearance** panel and click the **Add new effect** icon.

7. In the menu that appears, click on the **Brush Strokes** category and click on **Sumi-e**.

8. This effect paints an image in Japanese style as if were a wet brush full of black ink on rice paper, and it is even more spectacular than the one you previously applied. In the Effect Options box, you can modify the stroke width, pressure, and contrast. In this case, and given that your image contains quite a lot of black, decrease the contrast value using the corresponding slider  and click on **OK** to apply the effect.

9. Finish the exercise by deselecting the picture and saving the changes.

Applying pixelate and sketch effects

PIXELATE EFFECTS SHARPLY DEFINE a selection by clumping pixels of similar color values, whereas Sketch effects add texture to images, often for a 3D effect.

1. In this exercise dedicated to the application of effects on images in Illustrator, you will practice with two different effect categories: the Pixelate and the Sketch effects. You will work on the image of the panda bear from the previous exercise, but as you know, you can practice on any other image. Select the image from the artwork.

2. You will undo the last applied effect of the previous exercise from the **Appearance** panel. Open the panel, select the effect name, and click on the icon that displays a trash bin to remove it.

3. Now the image has no applied effect. Open the **Effect** menu, click on the **Pixelate** command and select the **Pointillize** effect from the list.

4. The **Pointillize** dialog box opens, where the only parameter that can be modified is the cell size, which is to say, the size of the points. This size is very small by default, but you can

094

increase it to the size you prefer. Try it out: drag the slider to the right of the field and check the result in the preview.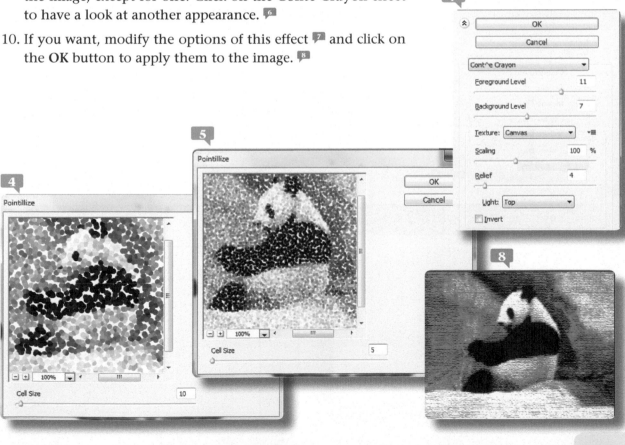

5. Note that the larger the points are, the harder it is to identify the contents of the image. Therefore, enter the value 5 (the default in the **cell size** field) and press the **OK** button to apply the effect.

6. This effect breaks up the color in an image into randomly placed dots, as in a pointillist painting, and uses the background color as a canvas area between the points. Discard the effect to give you an example of a sketch effect. Press the key combination **Ctrl + Z**.

7. Open the **Effect** menu and click on the **Sketch** command.

8. Many of the fourteen available effects in this category use black and white colors to redraw the image. As an example, click on the **Bas Relief** effect.

9. As you can see in the window of the chosen effect, all effects of the **Sketch** category are based on black and white to modify the image, except for one. Click on the **Conté Crayon** effect to have a look at another appearance.

10. If you want, modify the options of this effect and click on the **OK** button to apply them to the image.

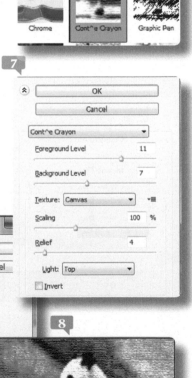

Adding texture effects

TEXTURE EFFECTS, INCLUDED IN ILLUSTRATOR among the Photoshop effects, give images an appearance of depth, substance, or add an organic look.

1. In this exercise, you will work with some of the texture effects in Illustrator. In this case, you will apply the effects to the background of the illustration **Tomatoes3.ai**. This is a new version of the **Tomatoes.ai** file, which you can download from our website, where a new layer with a white rectangle as a background artwork has been traced. After copying the file to your images or document folder, open it in Illustrator.

2. Click on an empty area of the artwork to select the rectangle with the white fill that will be your background.

3. Open the **Effect** menu, click on the **Texture** command and click on the **Mosaic Tiles** effect in the submenu.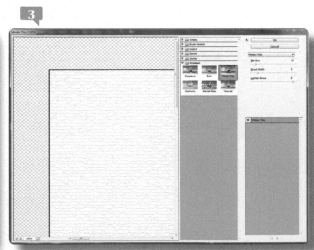

4. The temporary application progress of the effect on the artwork is a little longer since the application surface is larger (for example compared to an image). When you finish, the effect window opens displaying only a part of the selected background in the preview area.  The **Mosaic Tiles** effect

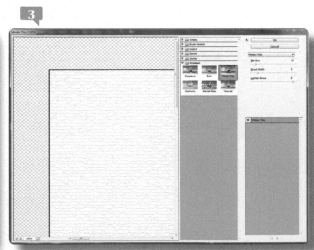

contains three custom parameters: tile size, width, and grout clarification. Grout is the material used in the space between the tiles. Use the scroll bars to increase these values slightly.

5. Observe the change in the preview area. (You can move the background in this preview or reduce the zoom to see more pieces.) Here is another texture option: in the center panel of this window, click on the effect called **Craquelure**.

6. With Craquelure you can change the space, depth, and brightness. Then click on the **Patchwork** effect.

7. In this case, the size of each square that makes up the texture and the relief are custom values. Now click on the **Stained Glass** effect.

8. Since this will be the effect you will apply as a background, you will customize some of the parameters. You will decrease the border width. Type the value **2** in this field.

9. You will keep the remaining options as they appear by default. Click on **OK** to apply the texture to the background of the artwork.

10. Make sure to practice on your own and try out the different available texture effects on your artwork.

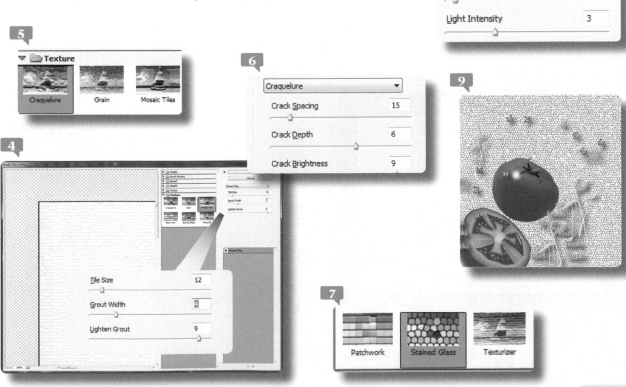

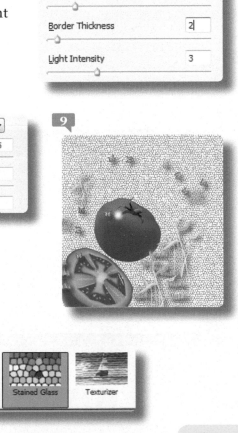

Using distort effects

DISTORT EFFECTS GEOMETRICALLY DISTORT an image and allow you to manipulate it in different aspects. They are similar to the aspects used in the Distort and Transform commands.

IMPORTANT

Keep in mind that the effects included in the **Distort** category in the **Effect** menu are very memory-intensive, so you need to be cautious when using them in your artwork.

Distort
Pixelate
Sketch
Stylize

1. In this exercise, you will learn about the different distort effects and how they can change the appearance of an image. To do this, and given that your images are already quite manipulated, you will create a new document and insert a new image that can be downloaded from our website, which is called **Draw.bmp**. However, as always you can use any other image you have stored on your computer in this format. Create a new document and place it in the center of the above-mentioned image.

2. Once the image is opened in the document, embed it by pressing the **Embed** button in the **Options Bar.**

3. Select the embedded image. Open the **Effect** menu and click on the **Distort** command.

4. The **Distort** category only contains three effects, so you can try out the appearance and the result of all of them. Click on the **Glass** effect.

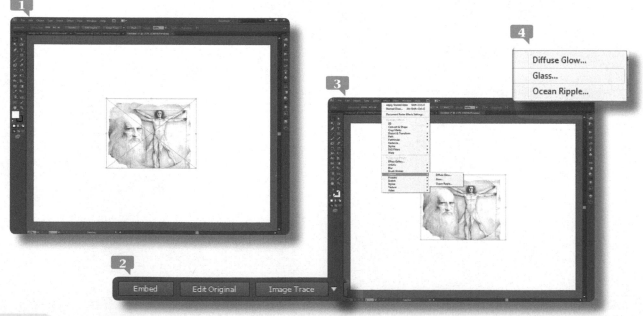

096

5. The window of the selected effect opens. In this case, the distortion consists of a glass layer on the image. The degree of distortion can be modified in the right part of this window, as well as the smoothness, texture, and scaling. The default texture is called **Frosted**. Look at some of the options. Open this field. 5

6. Try out all available textures, then select **Blocks** 6 and press **OK** to apply the distortion. 7

7. Press the key combination **Ctrl + Z** to undo the effect application.

8. Reopen the **Effect** menu, click on the **Distort** command, and this time select the **Ocean Ripple** effect.

9. The distortion of this effect is quite exaggerated, but it can be reduced with the ripple size and ripple magnitude controls. Try it out. Enter the value **2** in the **Ripple Magnitude** field. 8

10. With this value the original image can be guessed better. Have a look at the appearance of the third and last distort effect. Click on the **Diffuse Glow** effect in the center panel of this window. 9

11. In this case, the Glow amount provides more or less visibility. Further, the colors of the image play an important role while applying effects. Decrease the Glow amount and click on **OK** to apply the effect. 10

IMPORTANT

The **Scaling** field in the Glass distort effect field can increase or decrease the distorted area. By default, it is set to 100%, but it can be increased up to 200%.

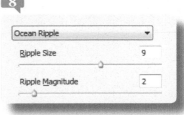

Applying light to a 3D object

IMPORTANT

If apart from applying lighting to 3D objects, you add a **shading** effect to them with the help of the appropriate effect in the Effect menu, you will obtain a tremendously realistic result.

BY DEFAULT, THE EFFECTS in the 3D category of the Effect menu apply lighting to an object. However, it is possible to add and remove lighting, taking into account that the object always needs to have at least one light.

1. In previous exercises, you have had the opportunity to create a 3D object from a 2D one. You saw how to change certain properties, but you did not practice with the lighting application. In this exercise, you will recreate a 3D object with the help of the **Effect** menu, and you will learn how to add light. Select the **Star Tool** in the **Tools** panel and draw this figure in a free area of the artwork.

2. Once you have prepared the figure, select it, open the **Effect** menu, click on the **3D** command and select the **Extrude & Bevel** effect.

3. The **3D Extrude & Bevel Options** box opens. Click on the **More Options** button in this box to display the lighting options at the bottom.

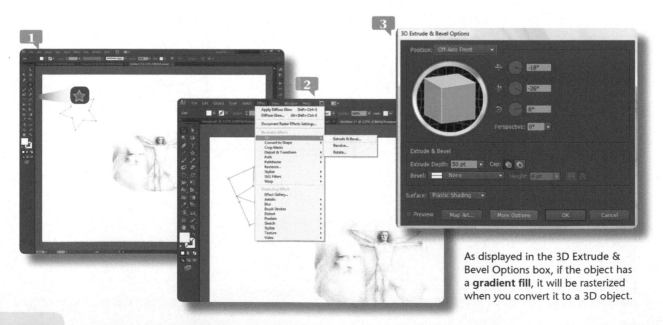

As displayed in the 3D Extrude & Bevel Options box, if the object has a **gradient fill**, it will be rasterized when you convert it to a 3D object.

4. In the **Surface** section, you can find the lighting options. The sphere displays the default light spot that can be moved to place it wherever you want. Click on the symbol above the sphere and move it with the help of the drag technique. 4

5. Enable the **Preview** option to check the effect of the modifications on the image.

6. The first button below the sphere allows you to move the selected light behind and in front of the object according to its current position. Click on this button and have a look at the result on the sphere. 5

7. The second button allows you to add new light to the object. Click on it. 6

8. By default, the new light is positioned in front of the sphere. Drag it to the top right part of the object. 7

9. The parameters on the right allow you to modify the light intensity, ambient light, the highlight intensity, and size as well as the blend steps. The Blend Steps control how smoothly the shading appears across the object's surface. Higher numbers produce smoother shades and more paths than lower numbers. Enter a value between 1 and 256. Change this value according to your preferences. 8

10. Click on **OK** to apply the 3D effect and the light to the object, 9 deselect it and save the changes. 10

097

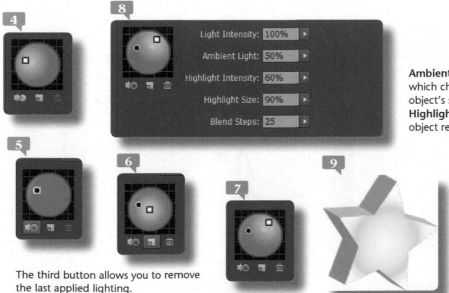

Ambient Light controls the global lighting, which changes the brightness of all the object's surfaces uniformly, whereas the **Highlight Intensity** controls how much the object reflects light.

The third button allows you to remove the last applied lighting.

Exporting artwork to Flash

SWF IS A VECTOR-BASED GRAPHICS FORMAT for interactive, animated Web graphics. Illustrator allows you to export your artwork to Flash format (SWF) for use in web design and view them in any browser equipped with the Flash Player plug-in.

1. In this exercise, you will learn how to export an artwork created with Illustrator to Flash. You will export the document **Project5.ai**, which contains tagged text. This way you can see that the text is working properly. With this illustration on the screen, open the **File** menu and click on the **Export** command.

2. This opens the **Export** dialog box where you have to choose the location of the new file and the format. By default the first file type from the list is selected. Display the **Save as type** field and select the **Flash (*SWF)** format.

3. The program uses the same name for the new document and the original illustration, and as a target location it determines the **Documents** folder. Modify these settings if you want and click on **Save**.

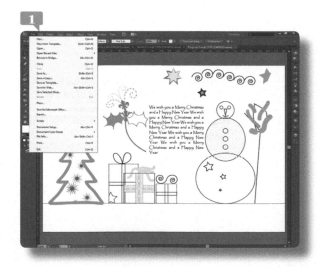

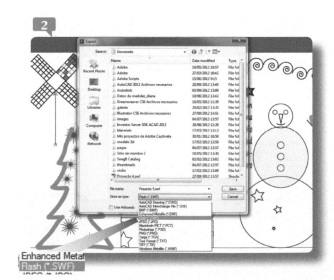

4. This opens the **SWF Options** dialog box, where you can configure various options for exporting the file. Set these options according to your preferences and click on **Web Preview**.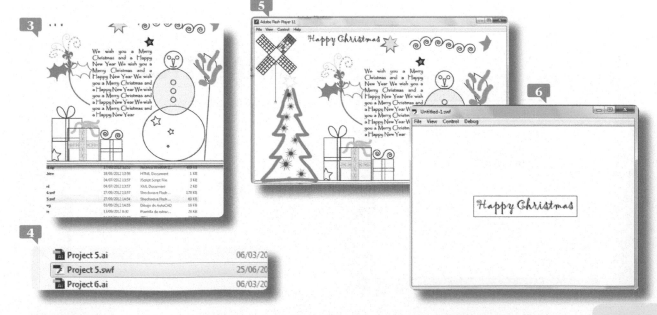

5. Your default web browser opens displaying the artwork. Close the program by clicking on the X of the **title bar**.

6. Go back to the SWF Export Options box and press **OK** to create the Flash file.

7. Open the file in Flash Player and check that the text works properly. Access the folder where you have stored the SWF file and open it.

8. Adobe Flash Player opens, displaying the artwork. The text edges are dynamic and the mouse cursor converts to the shape of a hand as you place the cursor on it to indicate that this is a link. Close Adobe Flash Player.

9. Illustrator also allows you to export text or objects to Flash using the traditional method of cut/copy and paste. Therefore, open both applications. Select the text and press the key combination **Ctrl + C**.

10. Place Flash with a new blank document in the foreground and press the key combination **Ctrl + V**.

11. Press the key combination **Ctrl + Enter** to test the movie and to make sure that when you click on the text, the web page, which was indicated when tagging the text for Flash, opens up.

Creating Flash animations in Illustrator

SWF IS A VECTOR-BASED GRAPHICS FORMAT for interactive, animated Web graphics. Illustrator allows you to export your artwork to Flash format (SWF) for use in web design and view the artwork in any browser equipped with the Flash Player plug-in.

1. In this exercise, you will learn how to create a simple animation using Illustrator CS6. To do this, open a new blank file and use the **Type Tool** to type the word **ANIMATION**, for example.

2. Edit the word, select a font type, color, and appearance you prefer. In this case, you will use a blue color and vary the size by pulling the handles and clicking on the **Shift** key to keep the proportions.

3. Press the **Alt** key and drag the word to copy it to the most appropriate position in order to blend it. Change the color. Repeat this procedure until you have written the word three times.

4. Click on any empty place on the screen to deselect the text and select the **Blend Tool.**

5. Double-click on the **Blend Tool** and select the **Specified Steps** option. Enter a high value between 20 and 30. Once this value is modified, press **OK**. 5

6. Click on the first word with the **Blend Tool**, then on the second and finally on the third. You can now see that many intermediate steps have been created. 6

7. After creating the design, open the **File** menu and select the **Export** option. 7 When you open the dialog box, select the file type **Flash (*SWF)**, rename your file and click on **Save** to save the file in Flash. Like that you have alreay created your first animation.

8. The SWF Options box opens. Select the basic level, choose a background color, and make sure that you have enabled the **Export as: AI Layers to SWF frames** option. Select the advanced level, click on **Looping** if you want to repeat the animation, and select **Animate Blends** in any of the two options. You can also modify the rate of appearance by changing the **Frame Rate**. 8

9. In the lower left corner you see the **Web preview** icon. Click on it to preview it and carry out the appropriate changes. Once you are satisfied, click on **OK** to create the Flash file.

10. You can always modify the original design and export the file to Flash again. In the download area, you will find the file **Animation.swf** to have a look at the animation effect.

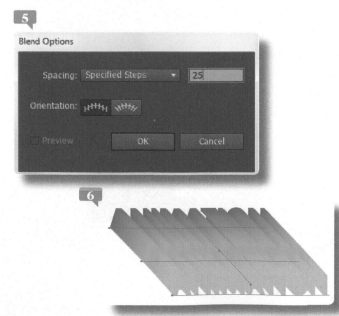

Creating PDF files

PDF IS A UNIVERSAL FILE FORMAT that preserves the fonts, images, and layout of source documents created on a wide range of applications and platforms. Moreover, PDF/X is a subset of Adobe PDF that eliminates many of the color, font, and trapping variables that lead to printing problems.

1. In this exercise, you will learn how to create different types of PDF files in Illustrator. Your goal is to create a single document that contains some of the illustrations with which you have been working in this book. Start the process with the illustration **Cover.ai**. Open the **File** menu and click on the **Save As** command. 1️⃣

2. This opens the **Save As** dialog box, in which you need to specify the file type you want to use to save the artwork, location, and name. By default, the specified location is the **Documents** folder and the name is the one you have assigned to the artwork in Illustrator. Open the **Save as type** field and select the **Adobe PDF** option. 2️⃣

3. Change the location and the name of the document if you want and press the **Save** button. 3️⃣

Besides the **Save As** command, you can also use the **Save a Copy** command.

4. The **Save Adobe PDF** dialog box opens, where you have to set the options you prefer. Check the option **View PDF after Saving** to have a look at the result as you finish the process.

5. Adjust the other options as you prefer and click on **Save PDF** to create the new document.

6. Remember that in order to read the PDF document, you need to have the free Adobe Reader software or Adobe Acrobat. At the end of the process, the document opens in one of those programs, as you have indicated in the Options Box. What you will do next is add the remaining Illustrator documents that are available. However, you should first save them all as PDFs by following the steps described previously. When you are done doing this, click on the arrow tip of the **Create** command and select the **Combine Files into a Single PDF** option.

7. In the **Combine Files** box, click on the arrow tip of the **Add Files** command, click on that option and select in the opening box the PDF files of Illustrator.

8. Go back to the **Combine Files** box, and click on the button of the same name to create a multipage PDF with these files.

9. Name the file **Project** and click on **Save**.

IMPORTANT

If you want to create a multipage PDF document, you need to work with artboards. In this case, you can check the Use Artboard option in the Save As box and even specify the number of boards or pages you want to print.

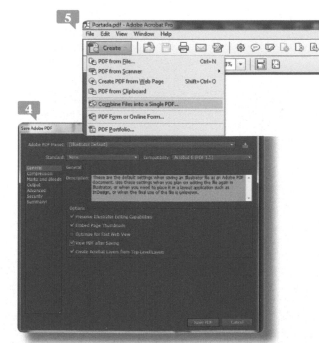

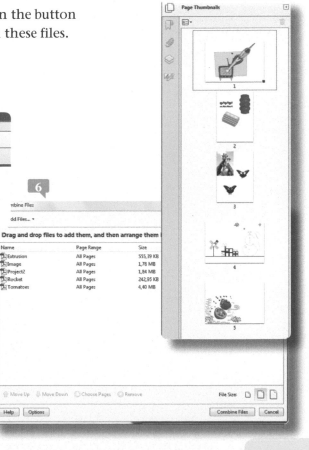

213

To continue learning...

This book is part of a collection that covers the most commonly used and known software in all professional areas.

All the books in the collection share the same aproach as the one you have just finished. So, if you would like to know more about the new features of Illustrator CS6 or other software packages, on the next page, you will find other books in this collection.

IMAGE RETOUCH

If you are interested in photo retouching, then 'Learning Photoshop CS6 with 100 practical exercises' is, without a doubt, the book that you are looking for.

Photoshop is the preeminent photo editor and image processing tool. In this new CS6 version of Photoshop, which is the subject of this book, Adobe has included interesting and spectacular developments that improve and facilitate the flow of work and increase image editing possibilities.

With this book, you will learn:

- Use the new Crop in Perspective Tool.
- Retouch images with incredible features such as Fill According to Content and the new Content-Aware Patch Tool.
- Transform certain parts of an image.
- Manage the layers of your documents more easily with the improvements in the Layers Panel.

PAGE LAYOUT

If you are interested in the layout of books and magazines, then your ideal book would be *Learning InDesign CS6 with 100 practical exercises.*

InDesign is the preeminent program for digital editing and layout. With this manual, you will learn how to use it easily. In this version of InDesign, Adobe has included some very interesting innovations that facilitate the handling of tools, mobility between sheets and documents, and insertion of images.

Within this book, you will learn to:

- Quickly design attractive compositions for digital editing and printing.
- Create interactive PDF documents.
- Create complex documents with cross-references, numbering, and bullets.
- Get to know your creative possibilities and create elegant page layouts.

COLLECTION LEARNING... WITH 100 PRACTICAL EXERCISES

IN PREPARATION...

DESIGN AND ASSISTED CREATIVITY

- Dreamweaver CS6
- Flash CS6
- Windows 8
- Image Retouch with Photoshop CS6
  with 100 practical exercises

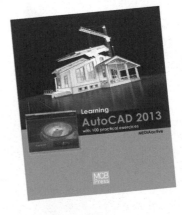